COMPLETE COOKERY

············

IN COLOUR

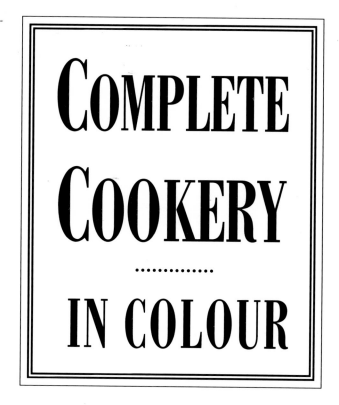

COMPLETE COOKERY

IN COLOUR

CHANCELLOR
PRESS

Inside photography by
Martin Brigdale: pages 183, 184 and 187
James Jackson: pages 2/3, 8/9, 26/27, 40/41, 58/59, 92/93, 108/109
120/121, 130/131, 144/145, 154/155, 164/165, 178/179
Paul Kemp: pages 11, 23, 29, 33, 64, 82, 85, 88–90, 106, 137
148, 153
John Lee: pages 13–15, 18–22, 30, 31, 43, 44, 46, 47, 52–56,
61-63, 66, 70, 71, 76 (right hand picture), 77, 83, 87, 95, 98,
99, 101, 104, 105, 112, 114, 123, 140, 141, 149, 157,
169 (left hand picture)
David Levin: pages 25, 101 and 160
Fred Mancini: pages 171, 174 (right hand picture), 175 and 176
Vic Paris: page 36
Paul Williams: pages 16, 34, 35, 38, 45, 49, 50, 65, 67, 68, 72,
86, 102, 111, 113, 115, 134, 135, 139, 142, 147, 150, 151, 158,
159, 162 and 163

The authors and publishers would like to thank the following
for supplying or sponsoring photographs:
International Magazine Service (page 37)
Pasta Information Centre (page 118)
Mazola Corn Oil (page 124)
Swiss Cheese Union (page 126)
Farmhouse English Cheese (page 128)
H. P. Bulmer Limited (Cider Makers) Hereford (page 129)

Previously published in 1988 by
The Hamlyn Publishing Group Limited
part of Reed International Books

This 1992 edition published by
Chancellor Press
Michelin House, 81 Fulham Road
London SW3 6RB

This collection of recipes was originally published
under the title *Hamlyn Best Recipes*

ISBN 1 85152 201 8

Printed in Hong Kong

Contents

Useful Facts and Figures

Notes on metrication

In this book quantities are given in metric and Imperial measures. Exact conversion from Imperial to metric measures does not usually give very convenient working quantities and so the metric measures have been rounded off into units of 25 grams. The table below shows the recommended equivalents.

Ounces	Approx g to nearest whole figure	Recommended conversion to nearest unit of 25
1	28	25
2	57	50
3	85	75
4	113	100
5	142	150
6	170	175
7	198	200
8	227	225
9	255	250
10	283	275
11	312	300
12	340	350
13	368	375
14	396	400
15	425	425
16 (1 lb)	454	450
17	482	475
18	510	500
19	539	550
20 ($1\frac{1}{4}$ lb)	567	575

Note: When converting quantities over 20 oz first add the appropriate figures in the centre column, then adjust to the nearest unit of 25. As a general guide, 1 kg (1000 g) equals 2.2 lb or about 2 lb 3 oz. This method of conversion gives good results in nearly all cases, although in certain pastry and cake recipes a more accurate conversion is necessary to produce a balanced recipe.

Liquid measures The millilitre has been used in this book and the following table gives a few examples.

Imperial	Approx ml to nearest whole figure	Recommended ml
$\frac{1}{4}$ pint	142	150 ml
$\frac{1}{2}$ pint	283	300 ml
$\frac{3}{4}$ pint	425	450 ml
1 pint	567	600 ml
$1\frac{1}{2}$ pints	851	900 ml
$1\frac{3}{4}$ pints	992	1000 ml (1 litre)

Spoon measures All spoon measures given in this book are level unless otherwise stated.

Can sizes At present, cans are marked with the exact (usually to the nearest whole number) metric equivalent of the Imperial weight of the contents, so we have followed this practice when giving can sizes.

Oven temperatures

The table below gives recommended equivalents.

	°C	°F	Gas Mark
Very cool	110	225	$\frac{1}{4}$
	120	250	$\frac{1}{2}$
Cool	140	275	1
	150	300	2
Moderate	160	325	3
	180	350	4
Moderately hot	190	375	5
	200	400	6
Hot	220	425	7
	230	450	8
Very hot	240	475	9

Notes for American and Australian users

In America the 8-fl oz measuring cup is used. In Australia metric measures are now used in conjunction with the standard 250-ml measuring cup. The Imperial pint, used in Britain and Australia, is 20 fl oz, while the American pint is 16 fl oz. It is important to remember that the Australian tablespoon differs from both the British and American tablespoons; the table below gives a comparison. The British standard tablespoon, which has been used throughout this book, holds 17.7 ml, the American 14.2 ml, and the Australian 20 ml. A teaspoon holds approximately 5 ml in all three countries.

British	American	Australian
1 teaspoon	1 teaspoon	1 teaspoon
1 tablespoon	1 tablespoon	1 tablespoon
2 tablespoons	3 tablespoons	2 tablespoons
$3\frac{1}{2}$ tablespoons	4 tablespoons	3 tablespoons
4 tablespoons	5 tablespoons	$3\frac{1}{2}$ tablespoons

An Imperial/American guide to solid and liquid measures

Solid measures

IMPERIAL	AMERICAN
1 lb butter or margarine	2 cups
1 lb flour	4 cups
1 lb granulated or caster sugar	2 cups
1 lb icing sugar	3 cups
8 oz rice	1 cup

Liquid measures

IMPERIAL	AMERICAN
$\frac{1}{4}$ pint liquid	$\frac{2}{3}$ cup liquid
$\frac{1}{2}$ pint	$1\frac{1}{4}$ cups
$\frac{3}{4}$ pint	2 cups
1 pint	$2\frac{1}{2}$ cups
$1\frac{1}{2}$ pints	$3\frac{3}{4}$ cups
2 pints	5 cups ($2\frac{1}{2}$ pints)

Note: When making any of the recipes in this book, only follow one set of measures as they are not interchangeable.

Soups and Starters

The first course can make or mar the meal, so select a tempting recipe to complement the main dish and arouse the appetite. Serve the starter, attractively garnished, with crusty bread, crisp toast or hot fresh rolls.

Stuffed Eggs, Melon Cocktail, Mushroom Cocktail
and Mixed Hors d'Oeuvre

Mixed Hors d'Oeuvre

(ILLUSTRATED ON PREVIOUS PAGE)

Arrange a selection of sliced cooked sausages – salami, various German sausages and liver sausage – on a platter with neat rows of sliced or quartered hard-boiled eggs, coated with a little mayonnaise, sliced tomatoes, cucumbers, peppers and onions. Add, if you like, some cooked whole prawns, flaked tuna fish or smoked mackerel. Serve a salad dressing made from 4 tablespoons oil, 2 tablespoons wine vinegar, seasoning, sugar and mustard to taste. Bread rolls or thinly sliced bread and butter can be served as an accompaniment.

Melon Cocktail

Bridget Jones

(ILLUSTRATED ON PREVIOUS PAGE)

1 small honeydew melon
$\frac{1}{2}$ or $\frac{1}{4}$ water melon
a few mint sprigs
a little caster sugar

Halve the honeydew melon and scoop out the seeds. Use a melon scoop to remove the flesh in neat balls. Make the water melon flesh into balls, again removing the seeds.

Mix all the melon balls in a bowl and add the mint, then sprinkle with a little sugar and chill thoroughly. To serve, spoon the cocktail into glasses and decorate with the sprigs of mint. SERVES 4

Mushroom Cocktail

Bridget Jones

(ILLUSTRATED ON PREVIOUS PAGE)

225 g/8 oz small button mushrooms
4 tablespoons olive oil
2 tablespoons lemon juice
salt and pepper
1 small clove garlic, crushed
2 tablespoons chopped parsley
2 tablespoons finely chopped red pepper
4 spring onions, finely chopped

Select small, even-sized mushrooms and trim the ends of the stalks. Mix the oil with the lemon juice and pour over the mushrooms. Toss well with seasoning and the remaining ingredients, then allow to marinate in a cool place for at least an hour.

Toss the mushrooms before serving them in small dishes or on a few crisp lettuce leaves. SERVES 4

Stuffed Eggs

Bridget Jones

(ILLUSTRATED ON PREVIOUS PAGE)

4 hard-boiled eggs
100 g/4 oz cream cheese
salt and pepper
1 tablespoon chopped fresh herbs
a selection of garnishes, for example stuffed
olives, smoked salmon rolls, bacon rolls,
anchovies, lumpfish roe, gherkins and fresh
herbs

Shell and halve the eggs, then scoop out and mash the yolks. Beat the cream cheese with the yolks, seasoning to taste and herbs. Pipe this mixture back into the egg whites and garnish neatly with colourful, well-flavoured ingredients.

The eggs can be served on a little green salad, or as part of a mixed hors d'oeuvre platter. SERVES 4

Breton Fish Soup

— Audrey Ellis —

225 g/8 oz cod or haddock fillet
300 ml/$\frac{1}{2}$ pint water
3 teaspoons lemon juice
1 stick celery, sliced
1 medium carrot, sliced
225 g/8 oz potatoes, sliced
1 medium onion, sliced
1 clove garlic, crushed
salt and pepper
25 g/1 oz butter
20 g/$\frac{3}{4}$ oz plain flour
300 ml/$\frac{1}{2}$ pint milk
2 tablespoons chopped parsley

Place the fish in a saucepan with the water, lemon juice, celery, carrot, potatoes, onion, garlic and seasoning. Bring to the boil, cover and cook gently for 20 minutes. Lift out the fish with a slotted spoon, remove the skin and roughly flake the flesh. Continue to cook the vegetables for a further 10 minutes, or until they are soft. Drain off and reserve the liquid.

Melt the butter in a large clean saucepan and stir in the flour. Gradually add the milk and reserved stock, bring to the boil, stirring, and cook for 2 minutes. Stir in the fish and the vegetable mixture and finally add the parsley. Taste and adjust the seasoning if necessary. Serve with fresh rolls. SERVES 4

Country Herbed Bread

— Audrey Ellis —

Slice a large crusty white loaf of bread (preferably a bloomer), cutting through almost to the bottom. Soften 175 g/6 oz butter, mash and season with salt, pepper, a crushed garlic clove and chopped fresh mixed herbs to taste. Spread this herb butter generously into the cuts in the bread. Press the slices together to re-form the loaf and wrap in foil. Place the bread in a moderately hot oven (190 C, 375 F, gas 5) for 15 minutes. Serve the slices, cut apart, in a napkin-lined basket. SERVES 6

Cream of Fennel Soup

Jill Spencer

2 heads of fennel (about 575 g/1¼ lb)
juice of ½ lemon
40 g/1½ oz butter
40 g/1½ oz plain flour
600 ml/1 pint chicken stock
300 ml/½ pint milk
½ teaspoon mace
salt and pepper
a little chopped parsley
fennel sprigs to garnish

Trim and wash the fennel, cut it into quarters and cook in boiling salted water with the lemon juice until tender – about 30 minutes.

Drain and roughly slice the fennel. Melt the butter in a large saucepan and sauté the fennel in it for a few minutes. Stir in the flour, then add half the stock and half the milk, the mace, seasoning and parsley. Purée the soup in a liquidiser or food processor, or by pressing it through a fine metal sieve.

Pour the soup back into the saucepan, add the remaining stock and milk, and bring to the boil. Simmer gently, stirring occasionally, for 10 to 15 minutes. Serve hot, garnished with a sprig of fennel. SERVES 4

French Onion Soup

Jill Spencer

50 g/2 oz butter
1 tablespoon oil
450 g/1 lb onions, finely sliced
a little chopped parsley
900 ml/1½ pints well-flavoured beef stock
1 teaspoon yeast extract
salt and pepper
4 slices French bread
100 g/4 oz cheese, grated

Melt the butter in a saucepan with the oil. Add the onions and stir well, then fry gently over a low heat until browned.

Add the parsley to the fried onions, with the stock, yeast extract and seasoning to taste. Bring to the boil, then reduce the heat and simmer the soup for 20 minutes.

While the soup is simmering, top the bread with plenty of grated cheese. When you are almost ready to serve the soup, toast the cheese until golden brown. Pour the soup into four individual bowls and place a piece of bread on top of each. SERVES 4

Tomato and Carrot Soup

Jill Spencer

50 g/2 oz butter
1 small onion, finely chopped
175 g/6 oz carrots, finely chopped
450 g/1 lb tomatoes, peeled and finely chopped
50 g/2 oz plain flour
1.15 litres/2 pints mixed herb or chicken stock
1 teaspoon caster sugar
1 teaspoon dried oregano
½ teaspoon paprika · ½ teaspoon mace
2 tablespoons tomato purée
salt and pepper
6 tablespoons single cream

Melt the butter in a saucepan and lightly sauté the chopped vegetables in it. Stir in the flour and add the stock, sugar, oregano, spices, tomato purée and seasoning, stirring continuously. Bring to the boil, reduce the heat and cover the pan, then simmer for 30 minutes.

Purée the soup in a liquidiser or food processor, or by pressing it through a fine sieve. Return the soup to the rinsed out saucepan and reheat to boiling point. Serve in individual bowls, with a tablespoon of single cream swirled into each portion. SERVES 4 TO 6

Oatmeal and Vegetable Soup

Rosemary Wadey

1 large onion, finely chopped
1 turnip, finely chopped
2 large carrots, chopped
1 large leek, trimmed, thinly sliced and washed
50 g/2 oz dripping or butter
25 g/1 oz medium oatmeal
900 ml/1½ pints chicken stock
salt and pepper · 450 ml/¾ pint milk

Sauté all the vegetables in the fat for about 5 minutes without browning. Stir in the oatmeal and continue cooking for a few minutes, stirring frequently. Pour in the stock and add seasoning, then bring to the boil. Cover the pan and simmer the soup for about an hour.

Add the milk, taste and adjust the seasoning, then bring back to the boil and cook for 3 to 4 minutes. SERVES 4 TO 6

Cream of Cauliflower Soup

Rosemary Wadey

50 g/2 oz butter
1 large onion, chopped
1 small cauliflower, trimmed and roughly
chopped
600 ml/1 pint chicken stock
600 ml/1 pint milk
salt and pepper
bay leaf
2 blades mace
150 ml/$\frac{1}{4}$ pint single cream
chopped parsley to garnish

Melt the butter in a saucepan and fry the onion in it until
soft. Reserve a few florets of cauliflower for garnish; add
the remaining florets to the onion and continue cooking
gently for 5 minutes. Pour in the stock and milk, and
bring to the boil. Season to taste, add the bay leaf and
mace, then cover the pan and simmer the soup for 30 to 40
minutes or until the cauliflower is tender. Discard the bay
leaf and mace at the end of the cooking time.

Sieve or liquidise the soup and return it to the pan.
Taste and adjust the seasoning, if necessary, and stir in
the cream, then reheat without boiling. Garnish with the
reserved cauliflower florets and the parsley, then serve
with melba toast (below). SERVES 6

Note: To make melba toast, lightly toast medium-thick
slices of bread on both sides. Working as quickly as you
can, before the toast cools and becomes crisp, cut off the
crusts and slice horizontally through the middle of each
piece of toast to give very thin slices. Place these under
the grill, untoasted side uppermost, and cook until the
toast curls and browns.

Borscht

Rosemary Wadey

450 g/1 lb uncooked beetroot, grated
2 carrots, chopped
1 onion, chopped
bay leaf
1.15 litres/2 pints chicken stock
salt and pepper
a little lemon juice
150 ml/$\frac{1}{4}$ pint soured cream

Put the beetroot in a saucepan with the carrots, onion,
bay leaf, stock and seasoning. Bring to the boil, cover the
pan and simmer for about 45 minutes. Strain the soup and
pour it back into the saucepan. Taste and adjust the
seasoning and sharpen the soup with lemon juice. Bring
back to the boil and serve, topping each portion with a
spoonful of soured cream. SERVES 6

Spinach Soup

Rosemary Wadey

25 g/1 oz butter
1 onion, finely chopped
1 clove garlic, crushed
4 rindless rashers lean bacon, finely chopped
1 (227-g/8-oz) packet frozen chopped spinach
2 tablespoons plain flour
900 ml/1½ pints chicken stock
salt and pepper · a little grated nutmeg
25 g/1 oz Cheddar cheese, finely grated

Melt the butter in a saucepan and gently fry the onion, garlic and bacon in it for 5 minutes. Add the spinach and continue to cook gently, stirring frequently, until it has thawed out. Stir in the flour, then gradually whisk in the stock. Bring to the boil and season to taste with salt, pepper and nutmeg. Cover the pan and simmer the soup for 25 to 30 minutes.

Either leave the soup as it is, or sieve or liquidise it if a smooth soup is preferred. Pour the soup back into the pan, bring back to the boil and taste and adjust the seasoning. Serve, sprinkled with cheese. SERVES 4 TO 6

Minestrone Soup

Rosemary Wadey

50 g/2 oz haricot beans
1.75 litres/3 pints chicken stock
3 tablespoons oil
25 g/1 oz butter
2 carrots, chopped
1 large onion, chopped
1 clove garlic, crushed
2 leeks, trimmed, thinly sliced and washed
1 (396-g/14-oz) can peeled tomatoes
1 tablespoon tomato purée
bouquet garni
salt and pepper
50 g/2 oz spaghetti, broken up
Parmesan cheese to serve

Soak the beans in 600 ml/1 pint of the stock overnight. The following day add a further 600 ml/1 pint of stock and simmer the beans gently for 1 hour.

Heat the oil with the butter in a saucepan. Fry the carrots, onion, garlic and leeks in this mixture until soft and just beginning to colour – about 5 minutes. Add the tomatoes, tomato purée, bouquet garni and simmered beans with any of their cooking liquid. Season to taste, then pour in the remaining stock and bring to the boil. Cover and simmer gently for 1 hour or until the beans are tender. Add the spaghetti and continue cooking for a further 10 to 15 minutes until tender.

Discard the bouquet garni, taste and adjust the seasoning if necessary and serve, sprinkled with Parmesan cheese. SERVES 4 TO 6

Kipper Cocktail

1 (198-g/7-oz) can kipper fillets
150 ml/$\frac{1}{4}$ pint soured cream · $\frac{1}{2}$ lemon
1 tablespoon tomato ketchup
2 teaspoons French mustard
3 tablespoons mayonnaise
salt and pepper
2 large dessert apples
3 sticks celery
50 g/2 oz cashew nuts
parsley sprigs or celery leaves to garnish

Drain the canned kippers and cut them into small bite-sized pieces. Beat the soured cream until smooth and creamy. Grate the zest from the half lemon and add to the soured cream with the tomato ketchup, mustard and mayonnaise. Stir well to blend, then season to taste with salt and freshly ground black pepper.

Core the apples and cut them into small chunks. Put these in a bowl with the kippers and sprinkle with the juice squeezed from the half lemon. Clean and slice the celery and add it to the kipper and apple mixture together with half the nuts.

Pour the sauce over the kipper and apple mixture and toss so that the ingredients are lightly coated. Divide the mixture between six glasses, cover and chill them for at least 1 hour.

Serve the chilled cocktails sprinkled with the remaining nuts and garnished with parsley sprigs or celery leaves. SERVES 6

Taramasalata

Carol Bowen

100 g/4 oz smoked cod's roe, skin removed
4 slices white bread
about 3 tablespoons water
3 tablespoons lemon juice
200 ml/7 fl oz olive oil
1 small onion, finely grated
1 teaspoon chopped fresh dill (optional)
GARNISH
black olives · lemon slices

Soak the cod's roe in water for 5 minutes to remove some of the salt, then drain. Trim off and discard the crusts from the bread and soak the slices in the 3 tablespoons water for 2 minutes; remove and squeeze dry.

Place the cod's roe, bread, lemon juice, oil, onion and dill, if used, in a liquidiser and blend until smooth.

Alternatively, mash the roe, bread, onion and dill by hand with a fork. When smooth, blend in the lemon juice and olive oil slowly, stirring continuously, until well blended. Beat with a whisk until pink and creamy.

Chill before serving. Garnish with black olives and twists of lemon, if used. SERVES 4 TO 6

Gazpacho

Carol Bowen

3 small slices brown bread, cut into
2.5-cm/1-in cubes
600 ml/1 pint canned tomato juice
2 cloves garlic, finely chopped
$\frac{1}{2}$ cucumber, peeled and finely chopped
1 green pepper, deseeded and finely chopped
1 large onion, finely chopped
1 red pepper, deseeded and finely chopped
675 g/1$\frac{1}{2}$ lb tomatoes, peeled, seeds removed
and finely chopped
4 tablespoons olive oil
2 tablespoons red wine vinegar
$\frac{1}{2}$ teaspoon salt
$\frac{1}{4}$ teaspoon freshly ground black pepper
$\frac{1}{4}$ teaspoon dried marjoram
$\frac{1}{4}$ teaspoon dried basil
ice cubes (optional)
GARNISH
croûtons (see below)
chopped black or green olives
chopped cucumber
chopped green and red peppers
chopped onion

Place the bread cubes in a mixing bowl and pour in the tomato juice. Leave to soak for 5 minutes, then squeeze the bread to extract all the juice. Transfer the squeezed-out bread to a large mixing bowl and reserve the tomato juice.

Add the garlic, cucumber, green pepper, onion, red pepper and tomatoes to the bread and stir to mix, then purée the mixture in a liquidiser or by pressing it through a fine sieve. Stir in the reserved tomato juice.

Add the oil, vinegar, salt, pepper, marjoram and basil to the purée and mix well; the soup should be the consistency of single cream, so add more tomato juice if necessary.

Pour the soup into a deep tureen and chill for at least an hour. Just before serving, stir the soup well and float ice cubes on the surface, if you like. Serve with small bowls of croûtons, chopped olives, cucumber, peppers and onion. SERVES 4

Croûtons To make croûtons, fry small, neat cubes of bread in a mixture of oil and butter, turning them frequently, until golden brown all over. Drain on absorbent kitchen paper.

Vichyssoise

Rosemary Wadey

3 leeks
40 g/1½ oz butter
1 onion, thinly sliced
450 g/1 lb potatoes, chopped
900 ml/1½ pints chicken or veal stock
salt and pepper
pinch of grated nutmeg
1 egg yolk
150 ml/¼ pint single cream
chopped chives to garnish

Wash and trim the leeks, removing most of the green part, then finely slice the remainder. Melt the butter in a saucepan and fry the leeks and onion in it for 5 minutes without browning. Add the potatoes, stock, seasoning and nutmeg, and bring to the boil. Cover the pan and simmer the soup for about 30 minutes, or until the vegetables are soft.

Sieve or liquidise the soup, return it to the pan and reheat until it is almost boiling. Blend the egg yolk into the cream, then whisk into the soup and reheat gently without boiling. Adjust the seasoning, cool and chill thoroughly. Serve the soup sprinkled with the chives. SERVES 4 TO 6

Iced Lemon Soup

Rosemary Wadey

40 g/1½ oz butter
1 onion, chopped
1 clove garlic, crushed (optional)
25 g/1 oz plain flour
900 ml/1½ pints well-flavoured chicken stock
grated rind and juice of 1 large lemon
salt and pepper
bay leaf
300 ml/½ pint single cream
GARNISH
thin slices of lemon
mint sprigs

Melt the butter in a saucepan, add the onion and garlic and fry until soft but not browned. Stir in the flour, then gradually add the stock, stirring continuously, and bring to the boil. Add the lemon rind and juice, seasoning and bay leaf. Cover the pan, reduce the heat and simmer for 20 minutes.

Remove the bay leaf, sieve or liquidise the soup and pour it into a serving tureen or individual bowls. Stir in the cream and taste and adjust the seasoning. Cool, then chill thoroughly.

Garnish by floating thin slices of lemon in the soup, and top each portion with a sprig of mint. Serve with breadsticks. SERVES 6

Cucumber Soup

Rosemary Wadey

1 large cucumber, diced
900 ml/1½ pints chicken stock
2 tablespoons finely chopped onion
25 g/1 oz butter
20 g/¾ oz plain flour
salt and pepper
a little lemon juice
a little green food colouring (optional)
2 egg yolks
4 tablespoons single cream
GARNISH
mint sprigs
cucumber slices

Place the cucumber in a saucepan with the stock and onion. Bring to the boil, cover and simmer for about 20 minutes, or until the cucumber is tender. Cool, then sieve or blend in a liquidiser.

Melt the butter in a pan, stir in the flour and cook for 1 minute. Gradually add the cucumber purée. Bring to the boil, stirring frequently, simmer for 2 minutes, then season to taste with salt, pepper and lemon juice. Add a little green food colouring, if liked. Blend the egg yolks into the cream, then whisk in a little of the soup. Return this mixture to the pan and reheat gently, whisking continuously, but do not boil the soup. Cool and chill thoroughly. Serve garnished with mint sprigs and cucumber slices. SERVES 6

Chilled Avocado Soup

Rosemary Wadey

2 tablespoons finely chopped onion
40 g/1½ oz butter
25 g/1 oz plain flour
750 ml/1¼ pints chicken stock
2 ripe avocados
1-2 teaspoons lemon juice
salt and pepper
150 ml/¼ pint milk
150 ml/¼ pint single cream

Fry the onion gently in the butter for 3 to 5 minutes without allowing it to brown. Add the flour and cook for 1 minute. Gradually add the stock and bring to the boil, then simmer for 5 minutes. Quarter the avocados, remove the stones and peel. Cut off and reserve a few slices for garnish; dip these in a little lemon juice. Roughly chop the remaining avocado and add to the soup with the rest of the lemon juice and the seasoning. Simmer for 3 to 4 minutes to prevent the avocado from discolouring.

Sieve or blend in a liquidiser, stir in the milk and cream and adjust the seasoning. Cool, then chill thoroughly. Serve garnished with the reserved slices of avocado. SERVES 4

Prawn Soufflés

Diana Jaggar

20 g/¾ oz butter
1 teaspoon paprika
225 g/8 oz peeled prawns
a few drops of Tabasco sauce
salt and pepper
450 ml/¾ pint Béchamel sauce (below)
2 tablespoons single cream
2 tablespoons finely grated cheese
2 tablespoons browned breadcrumbs
3 egg yolks
4 egg whites

Melt the butter in a saucepan and add the paprika. Cook for 1 minute, then add the prawns, Tabasco, salt and pepper. Stir in the sauce and cream and allow the mixture to cool slightly. Mix the cheese and breadcrumbs and set aside.

Beat the egg yolks one at a time into the prawn mixture, making sure they are thoroughly incorporated. Whisk the egg whites until stiff but not dry and stir 1 tablespoon into the mixture, then carefully fold in the remainder. Spoon into six well-greased individual ovenproof soufflé dishes, place them on a baking sheet and sprinkle with the cheese and breadcrumb mixture. Bake in a moderate oven (180 c, 350 f, gas 4) for 20 to 25 minutes, until risen and crisp. Serve immediately. SERVES 6

Béchamel Sauce Melt 40 g/1½ oz butter in a saucepan. Stir in 40 g/1½ oz plain flour and cook for 1 minute. Gradually add 450 ml/¾ pint milk which has been infused with a bay leaf, a blade of mace and a slice of onion and then strained. Boil, cook for 2 minutes and season.

Sardine-stuffed Lemons

Rosemary Wadey

4 lemons
2 tablespoons soured cream
1 (120-g/4¼-oz) can sardines in oil, drained
and mashed
2 tablespoons finely chopped cucumber
1 tablespoon chopped capers
salt and pepper
dash of Tabasco sauce
1 small lettuce

Cut the tops off the lemons and cut a sliver from the base of each so that they stand. Scoop out the lemon flesh and squeeze 1 tablespoon of juice from it.

Mix together the soured cream, lemon juice, mashed sardines, cucumber and capers. Season to taste with salt, pepper and Tabasco. Spoon the mixture into the lemons, chill and serve on lettuce leaves. SERVES 4

Gratin au Fruits de Mer

Diana Jaggar

350 g/12 oz cod fillet, skinned and cut into
strips
100-175 g/4-6 oz peeled prawns
6 scallops, cut into quarters
juice of 1 lemon
salt and pepper
50 g/2 oz butter
1 small onion, finely chopped
100 ml/4 fl oz white wine
40 g/1½ oz plain flour
450 ml/¾ pint milk, infused with a bay leaf, a
blade of mace and a few peppercorns
25 g/1 oz Parmesan cheese, grated
a few parsley sprigs to garnish

Mix the cod strips, prawns and scallops with the lemon
juice and seasoning, then divide between six deep scallop
shells or ovenproof dishes.

Melt the butter in a saucepan, add the onion and cook
until soft, then add the wine and bring to the boil.
Simmer until reduced by half, whisk in the flour and
cook until smooth, stirring continuously. Strain in the
infused milk, bring back to the boil and simmer for 2 to 3
minutes. Taste and adjust the seasoning and spoon this
sauce over the fish to cover it completely. Sprinkle with
the cheese and bake at the top of a moderately hot oven
(190 C, 375 F, gas 5) for 20 to 30 minutes, or until golden
brown on top. Serve immediately, garnished with sprigs
of parsley. SERVES 6

Prawns Newburg

Rosemary Wadey

1 small onion, finely chopped
50 g/2 oz butter
225 g/8 oz peeled prawns
2 tablespoons lemon juice
4 tablespoons sherry or Madeira
salt and pepper
50 g/2 oz long-grain rice, cooked
2 egg yolks
150 ml/¼ pint single cream
watercress sprigs to garnish

Fry the onion in the butter until soft. Add the prawns and
cook gently for 5 minutes, shaking the pan frequently.
Stir in the lemon juice, sherry or Madeira and seasoning
and bring to the boil. Add the cooked rice and mix
thoroughly.

Beat the egg yolks into the cream and add to the pan.
Heat gently, stirring continuously, but do not allow to
boil. Adjust the seasoning and serve in small dishes,
garnished with the watercress. SERVES 4

Chicken Liver Pâté

Rosemary Wadey

1 onion, very finely chopped
1 or 2 cloves garlic, crushed
50 g/2 oz butter
450 g/1 lb chicken livers
salt and pepper
2 tablespoons double cream
2 tablespoons red wine
75 g/3 oz butter, melted
GARNISH
bay leaves · capers

Fry the onion and garlic in the butter until soft but not browned. Wash and drain the chicken livers, add to the pan and cook gently for 10 minutes, stirring occasionally to prevent them from sticking. Remove the pan from the heat and stir in the seasoning, cream and wine.

Sieve or liquidise the pâté, adjust the seasoning to taste and pack into six individual dishes. Garnish each with a small bay leaf and a few capers. Cover the tops with a thin layer of melted butter and chill thoroughly. SERVES 6

Farmhouse Pâté

Rosemary Wadey

175 g/6 oz pig's liver, cubed
175 g/6 oz stewing steak, cubed
175 g/6 oz lean belly pork, cubed
1 large onion, roughly chopped
1 or 2 cloves garlic, crushed
25 g/1 oz fresh white breadcrumbs
1 large egg, beaten
salt and pepper
generous pinch of grated nutmeg
3 or 4 tablespoons red or white wine
175 g/6 oz rindless streaky bacon
GARNISH
chopped red pepper
chopped cucumber

Coarsely mince the liver, steak, pork and onion. Add the garlic, breadcrumbs, egg, seasoning, nutmeg and wine, and mix thoroughly.

Stretch the bacon rashers by placing them on a board and running the blunt edge of a knife along them, pressing firmly. Line a 450-g/1-lb loaf tin with the streaky bacon and spoon the pâté mixture into the tin. Press down evenly and fold the ends of the bacon over the top. Stand the pâté in a roasting tin and pour in enough hot water to give a depth of 2.5 cm/1 in. Cook in a moderately hot oven (180c, 350F, gas 4) for 1½ to 2 hours. Place a weight on the top of the pâté, allow to cool and chill for several hours.

Serve cut into neat slices, garnished with chopped red pepper and cucumber, with hot toast and butter. SERVES 6 TO 8

Chicken Liver Terrine

Audrey Ellis

225 g/8 oz streaky bacon
225 g/8 oz chicken livers
100 g/4 oz pork sausagemeat
50 g/2 oz fresh white breadcrumbs
2 tablespoons lemon juice
grated rind of 1 lemon
175 g/6 oz cooked chicken meat, diced
salt and pepper

Remove the rind from the bacon and stretch the rashers with the back of a knife. Use to line a 450-g/1-lb loaf tin.

Finely chop the chicken livers and combine them with the sausagemeat. Soak the breadcrumbs in the lemon juice for a few minutes, then work evenly into the sausagemeat mixture, adding the lemon rind. Press half this mixture into the prepared tin, then cover it with the diced chicken. Season generously and top with the remaining sausagemeat mixture. Press the sausagemeat down evenly using the back of a metal spoon. Cover the tin with greased foil and stand it in a roasting tin half-filled with warm water. Cook in a moderate oven (180 C, 350 F, gas 4) for 1¾ hours.

Allow to cool, and leave until the terrine shrinks away from the sides of the tin. Turn out and serve with crusty French bread. SERVES 4 TO 6

Pork and Olive Pâté

Jane Todd

4 spring onions, chopped
450 g/1 lb minced pork
225 g/8 oz sausagemeat
1 tablespoon chopped fresh sage
12 pimiento-stuffed olives, sliced
salt and pepper
4 tablespoons dry cider
GARNISH
tomato slices
chopped parsley

Mix together the spring onions, pork, sausagemeat, sage and olives, adding plenty of seasoning. Bind the mixture with the cider and pack it into a greased 450-g/1-lb loaf tin. Cook the pâté in a moderate oven (180 C, 350 F, gas 4) for 1¼ hours.

Place a weight on the pâté and leave to cool in the tin. Chill for several hours. Turn out on to a serving dish and garnish with tomato slices and a sprinkling of chopped parsley. Serve with toast or French bread. SERVES 6

Brandied Turkey Mousse

Carol Bowen

1 (70-g/2½-oz) packet aspic jelly powder
600 ml/1 pint boiling turkey or chicken stock
225 g/8 oz cooked, boned smoked turkey,
finely diced
1 tablespoon tomato purée
1 teaspoon dried tarragon
2 egg yolks
250 ml/8 fl oz double cream
100 ml/4 fl oz brandy
salt and pepper
a few lettuce leaves
1 head chicory, separated into leaves
orange wedges to garnish

Place the aspic in a small bowl. Gradually add the stock, whisking well to dissolve the aspic powder. Cool.

Place all the ingredients except the lettuce leaves and chicory in a liquidiser and blend until smooth and creamy. Turn into a 1.15-litre/2-pint fluted mould and chill until set.

To serve, line a serving plate with the lettuce leaves. Turn the mousse out on to the plate and arrange the chicory leaves around the edge. Garnish with orange wedges and serve. SERVES 4

Asparagus and Parma Ham Rolls

Carol Bowen

1 (275-g/10-oz) can asparagus tips
salt and pepper
2 tablespoons mayonnaise
5 thin slices Parma ham
chopped parsley to garnish (optional)

Drain the asparagus tips and trim off the ends of the stalks to give 7.5-cm/3-in lengths. Finely chop the trimmings, season well and fold into the mayonnaise.

Sandwich four asparagus tips together using a little of the mayonnaise mixture and roll them up in a slice of Parma ham. Repeat with the remaining slices of ham. Place on a serving dish and garnish with chopped parsley, if used. MAKES 5.

Lamb Meatballs with Cream and Caraway Dip

Jane Todd

450 g/1 lb minced lamb
2 teaspoons ground cumin
3 teaspoons chopped fresh mint
2 spring onions, chopped
salt and pepper
25 g/1 oz fresh white breadcrumbs
1 egg, lightly beaten
CREAM AND CARAWAY DIP
300 ml/½ pint soured cream
1 teaspoon caraway seeds

Mix together the lamb, cumin, mint, spring onions, seasoning and breadcrumbs, then bind the mixture with the lightly beaten egg. Flour your hands and shape the mixture into 2.5-cm/1-in meatballs. Place them in a greased roasting tin and cook in a hot oven (220 C, 425 F, gas 7) for 15 minutes or until well browned.

Meanwhile make the dip: mix the soured cream and caraway seeds. Spoon the dip into a serving bowl placed on a large plate or tray. Arrange the meatballs around the bowl. Serve cocktail sticks to spear the meatballs for dunking into the dip. MAKES ABOUT 30

Edam Dip

Jane Todd

1 whole Dutch Edam cheese
900 g/2 lb curd cheese
4 tablespoons soured cream
6 tablespoons chopped parsley or chives
2 teaspoons horseradish sauce
salt
paprika

Cut a slice from the top of the Edam cheese and serrate the edge in a zig-zag pattern using a sharp knife. With a melon baller, scoop out as many balls of cheese from the inside as possible. Using a teaspoon, hollow out the remaining cheese, leaving an empty shell. (These odd bits of cheese can be grated and used for other dishes.) Place the curd cheese in a bowl and beat with a wooden spoon to soften it. Mix in the soured cream, parsley or chives and horseradish sauce. Season well with salt and paprika.

Stand the Edam shell on a large platter and pile in the curd cheese mixture. Chill for about 30 minutes.

Serve surrounded with the scooped-out cheese balls, savoury biscuits and sticks of raw vegetables to dip into the cheese filling. SERVES UP TO 15

Meat Dishes

These meat recipes, ranging from simple Curried Minced Lamb
to expensive Beef Wellington, are intended to inspire you to
experiment with the cheaper cuts of meat as well as to attempt
an elaborate dinner party dish.

Pasta and Pepper Casserole, Orange-glazed Cutlets and
Pork and Apricot Kebabs

Fish and Seafood

Fish can be cooked in a multitude of ways to make light meals
or filling family fare. To extend your repertoire, here is a
selection of recipes ranging from simple fried fish to hearty
casseroles and light seafood moulds.

Lemon Seafood Bake, Fried Fish Fillets, Grilled Fish
and Baked Mackerel

Fried Fish Fillets

(ILLUSTRATED ON PREVIOUS PAGE)

Allow one or two fish fillets per person. Skin the fish if you like, then coat the fillets in a little seasoned flour. Dip each fillet in beaten egg, then coat each one in fine dry breadcrumbs, making sure that the fish is well covered to protect the flesh during cooking.

Fry the fillets, one or two at a time, in a little oil in a shallow frying pan. When the underside is golden, turn the fish and cook the second side. Drain on absorbent kitchen paper and serve immediately, garnished with wedges of lemon and parsley sprigs.

Grilled Fish

(ILLUSTRATED ON PREVIOUS PAGE)

Arrange fillets or steaks of fish on a foil-lined grill pan. Season to taste and add a few bay leaves if you like. Dot with butter or brush with a little oil. Cook under a moderate grill for 5 to 10 minutes. Turn the fish over and top with more seasoning and more oil or butter, then cook for a further 5 to 10 minutes.

Arrange the fish on a heated serving dish, or on individual plates, and pour the cooking juices on top. Garnish with lemon wedges, parsley or fresh bay leaves and serve immediately.

Lemon Seafood Bake

—— Bridget Jones ——

(ILLUSTRATED ON PREVIOUS PAGE)

450 g/1 lb cooked white fish
100 g/4 oz peeled prawns
100 g/4 oz button mushrooms, halved
4 scallops, cleaned
300 ml/$\frac{1}{2}$ pint dry white wine
salt and pepper
2 tablespoons chopped tarragon or parsley
grated rind of 1 lemon
300 ml/$\frac{1}{2}$ pint Béchamel Sauce (page 20)
GARNISH
halved lemon slices
parsley sprigs

Cut the fish into chunks, removing any bones and skin. Mix the fish with the prawns and mushrooms in an ovenproof dish. Poach the scallops in the wine with a little seasoning for 15 minutes, then remove them from the liquid and cut each one in half. Boil the cooking liquid until it is reduced to about a quarter of its original quantity. Place the scallops in the dish with the fish.

Stir the reduced cooking liquid, tarragon or parsley and lemon rind into the béchamel sauce. Pour over the fish mixture. Place in a moderately hot oven (200 c, 400 f, gas 6) for 20 to 30 minutes, or until lightly browned. Serve immediately garnished with the halved lemon slices and parsley sprigs. SERVES 4

Baked Mackerel

—— Bridget Jones ——

(ILLUSTRATED ON PREVIOUS PAGE)

4 small mackerel, cleaned
8 bay leaves
1 onion, sliced into rings
salt and pepper
75 g/3 oz butter *or* 2 tablespoons oil
lemon wedges to garnish

Leave the heads on the fish if you like. Rinse the body cavities and lay the fish on a large piece of greased cooking foil, on a baking tray. Place 2 bay leaves, a few onion rings and plenty of seasoning in each body cavity. Sprinkle seasoning over the top of the fish and dot generously with butter or sprinkle with the oil. Fold the foil around the fish and seal the edges together. Bake in a moderate oven (180 c, 350 f, gas 4) for 40 to 50 minutes, or until the fish is cooked through.

To serve, carefully lift the mackerel out of the foil and arrange them on a serving dish. Garnish with lemon wedges and the bay leaves and cooked onion. Serve immediately. SERVES 4

Tuna and Cod Cream

Audrey Ellis

15 g/½ oz gelatine
2 tablespoons water
1 (198-g/7-oz) can tuna, mashed
175 g/6 oz cooked cod, mashed
300 ml/½ pint mayonnaise
salt and pepper
1 (170-g/6-oz) can evaporated milk, chilled
1 tablespoon lemon juice
FILLING
2 teaspoons oil
2 teaspoons lemon juice
450 g/1 lb tomatoes, peeled and quartered
6 spring onions, chopped
GARNISH
radish slices
cucumber slices

Dissolve the gelatine in the water in a basin over a saucepan of hot water. Combine the tuna and oil from the can with the cod and mayonnaise, and season well. Stir in the dissolved gelatine. Whisk the evaporated milk with the lemon juice until thick, then fold it into the fish mixture. Pour into a 1.15-litre/2-pint ring mould or shallow dish and chill until set.

Mix together the oil and lemon juice for the filling and toss the tomatoes and spring onions in this dressing. Fill the centre of the turned-out ring with the tomato salad and serve garnished with radish and cucumber slices. If the mixture was set in a shallow dish, then arrange the tomato salad around the edge and place the slices of radish and cucumber on top. SERVES 4

Smoked Trout with Apple and Horseradish Cream

Carol Bowen

4 small smoked trout
1 lettuce heart, separated into leaves
4 parsley sprigs
1 lemon, cut into wedges
APPLE AND HORSERADISH CREAM
1 large cooking apple
1 tablespoon lemon juice
1 tablespoon horseradish sauce
3 tablespoons double cream or soured cream

Fillet the fish, if liked, then place the fillets on a dish lined with the lettuce heart. Cover the fish eyes with the parsley sprigs and garnish by placing lemon wedges between each fish.

Wash and quarter the apple, removing the core. Grate the apple, including the skin, on the coarse side of a grater. Add the lemon juice immediately to stop the apple flesh from discolouring. Stir in the horseradish sauce and the cream or soured cream, mixing well. Spoon into a sauceboat and serve with the smoked trout. SERVES 4

Cod à la Provençale

Julia Roles

450 g/1 lb tomatoes, peeled and chopped
rosemary sprig, chopped
2 thyme sprigs, chopped · salt and pepper
2 tablespoons white wine or water
3 shallots, chopped · 2 cloves garlic, crushed
2 tablespoons olive oil
675 g/1½ lb cod fillets
few drops of anchovy essence (optional)
chopped parsley to garnish

Place the tomatoes in a saucepan with the herbs, seasoning and wine or water. Bring to the boil, then cover and simmer gently for 15 minutes until soft and pulpy.

Meanwhile, sauté the shallots and garlic in the olive oil until softened. Lay the fish in the base of an ovenproof casserole and season lightly. Arrange the shallots on top. Add a few drops of anchovy essence to the tomato sauce, if liked, and pour over the fish. Cover and cook in a moderate oven (180 c, 350 f, gas 4) for 30 minutes. Serve, garnished with chopped parsley. SERVES 4

Smoked Haddock à la Russe

Julia Roles

675 g/1½ lb smoked haddock fillets
300 ml/½ pint dry white wine
salt and pepper · 25 g/1 oz butter
25 g/1 oz plain flour
½ small green pepper, deseeded and chopped
150 ml/¼ pint soured cream
GARNISH
star-shaped pieces of toasted bread
a few parsley sprigs

Place the haddock in a large frying pan with the wine and enough water to cover the fish. Season with pepper and bring to the boil, then lower the heat and simmer gently for 5 minutes. Drain the fish, reserving the cooking liquor, and cut it into chunks. Discard any skin and bones. Place in an ovenproof casserole.

Melt the butter in a saucepan and stir in the flour. Cook, stirring, for 1 minute, then remove from the heat and gradually blend in 300 ml/½ pint of the strained cooking liquor from the fish. Return to the heat and bring to the boil, stirring continuously. When the sauce is thick and glossy, add the chopped pepper and season to taste. Pour the sauce over the fish and mix well. Cover and cook in a moderate oven (180 c, 350 f, gas 4) for 20 minutes. Stir in the soured cream and return to the oven to heat through for a few minutes.

Garnish with the bread and parsley. SERVES 4 TO 6

Sole Véronique

Julia Roles

1 small onion, finely chopped
675 g/1½ lb sole or plaice fillets
salt and pepper
juice of ½ lemon
150 ml/¼ pint white wine
bay leaf
175 g/6 oz seedless white grapes, peeled
25 g/1 oz butter
25 g/1 oz plain flour
150 ml/¼ pint double cream
watercress sprigs to garnish

Sprinkle the onion over the base of a buttered ovenproof casserole. Fold the fish fillets in half and place them on top of the onion. Season to taste and add the lemon juice, wine, bay leaf and enough water to cover the fish. Cover the casserole and cook in a moderate oven (180 c, 350 f, gas 4) for 15 minutes. Reserve a few grapes for garnish and add the remainder to the dish. Return to the oven to heat through. Remove the fish and grapes from the sauce and keep hot. Discard the bay leaf.

Melt the butter in a saucepan, stir in the flour and cook for 1 minute. Remove from the heat and strain in the cooking liquid from the fish, made up to 300 ml/½ pint with extra wine or water. Bring to the boil, stirring, and cook until thick. Take off the heat, add the cream, heat through but do not boil.

Arrange the fish and grapes on a serving dish and pour the sauce on top. Garnish with the reserved grapes and watercress. SERVES 4

Sole Goujons

Moya Maynard

6−8 sole fillets, skinned
1 large egg
1 tablespoon water
salt and pepper
fresh breadcrumbs for coating
oil for deep frying

Cut the fish fillets diagonally into strips about 1 cm/½ in wide. Beat the egg with the water. Add salt and pepper. Spread the breadcrumbs on a sheet of greaseproof paper. Coat the fish strips in the egg, then toss in the breadcrumbs.

Heat the oil for deep frying to 180 c/350 f, add the goujons a few at a time and cook until crisp and golden. Drain on absorbent kitchen paper and serve with mixed salad and tartare sauce. SERVES 4

Moules Farcies Bretonne

Diana Jaggar

generous litre/2 pints large mussels
225 g/8 oz unsalted butter
1 large onion, finely chopped
3 cloves garlic, crushed
1 tablespoon chopped parsley
freshly ground black pepper
50 g/2 oz fresh white breadcrumbs
40 g/1½ oz Parmesan cheese, grated
100 ml/4 fl oz dry white wine

Wash and scrub the mussels well under cold running water. Remove the beards and discard any open shells. Place the mussels in a steamer or metal colander over a pan of boiling water. Cover closely with a lid and steam for 2 to 3 minutes, until the shells just open. Do not overcook the mussels. Stir occasionally to ensure that all the shells are steamed. Remove the pan from the heat and lift off the steamer. Break off and discard the empty half of each shell and place the halves with the mussels in on a board. Discard any mussels that do not open at all.

Cream the butter with the onion, garlic, parsley and pepper. Spread a little over each mussel in its shell and arrange close together in four small ovenproof gratin dishes or one large ovenproof dish. Mix the breadcrumbs with the cheese and sprinkle over the mussels. Pour in the wine and chill thoroughly.

Place the dish or dishes on a baking sheet and cover with foil. Cook for 15 to 20 minutes at the top of a moderate oven (180 C, 350 F, gas 4), remove the foil and continue cooking for a further 5 minutes to brown. Serve immediately with French bread. SERVES 4

Mixed Fish Chowder

Rosemary Wadey

2 rindless rashers lean bacon, chopped
1 onion, finely sliced
25 g/1 oz butter
1 (396-g/14-oz) can peeled tomatoes
750 ml/1¼ pints fish stock
bay leaf · salt and pepper
50 g/2 oz long-grain rice
225 g/8 oz cooked haddock or cod, flaked
100 g/4 oz peeled prawns
1 tablespoon chopped parsley
2 tablespoons single cream
a few whole prawns to garnish

Fry the bacon and onion in the butter until beginning to colour. Add the tomatoes, stock, bay leaf, seasoning and rice. Bring to the boil, cover and simmer for 20 minutes, or until the rice is cooked, stirring occasionally. Add the fish and prawns and continue cooking for 10 minutes.

Remove the bay leaf. Adjust the seasoning, stir in the parsley and cream, then serve, garnished with the whole prawns. SERVES 4 TO 6

Mediterranean Fish Casserole

Diana Jaggar

generous litre/2 pints mussels
450 g/1 lb cod steaks, skinned and cut into cubes
450 g/1 lb halibut, skinned and cut into cubes
a little seasoned flour
6 tablespoons oil
350 g/12 oz onions, halved and sliced
3 cloves garlic, crushed
350 g/12 oz tomatoes, peeled and quartered
1 teaspoon tomato purée
½ bottle dry white wine
juice of 1 lemon
pinch of dried thyme
½ teaspoon chopped fennel or dill
1 tablespoon chopped parsley
1 kg/2 lb cooked whole prawns
chopped parsley to garnish

Wash and scrub the mussels well under cold water. Remove the beards and discard any open shells. Toss the cod and halibut in a little seasoned flour. Heat 3 to 4 tablespoons of the oil in a frying pan and fry the fish until browned. Remove from the pan and add the remaining oil. Sauté the onions and garlic until the onion is soft but not browned. Add the tomatoes, tomato purée, white wine, lemon juice and herbs and bring to the boil.

Return the fish to the pan and simmer gently, covered, for 10 to 15 minutes until just cooked. Add the mussels, cover and leave for 3 to 4 minutes until they open. Discard any that do not open. Add the prawns and sprinkle with parsley before serving. SERVES 6

Devilled Mackerel

Audrey Ellis

2 tablespoons fresh white breadcrumbs
2 tablespoons grated onion
pinch of cayenne pepper
1 tablespoon dry mustard
4 mackerel, filleted
25 g/1 oz plain flour
50 g/2 oz butter
1 medium onion, sliced into rings

To make the stuffing, combine the breadcrumbs, grated onion, cayenne and half the mustard. Spread each mackerel fillet with a little of this stuffing and roll up. Secure each roll with a wooden cocktail stick. Mix the flour with the remaining mustard and use to coat the rolls.

Melt the butter in a large frying pan, add the fish rolls and fry over moderate heat for about 12 minutes, turning occasionally, until cooked through. Remove the cocktail sticks from the mackerel rolls and serve hot, topped with the onion rings. SERVES 4

Mackerel with Cider and Rosemary Marinade

Carol Bowen

4 medium mackerel, cleaned
150 ml/$\frac{1}{4}$ pint dry cider
2 tablespoons finely chopped fresh rosemary
salt and pepper
a few lettuce leaves
watercress sprigs to garnish

Cut about four deep diagonal slashes into each side of the mackerel. Place the fish in a shallow dish and pour over the cider. Sprinkle with the rosemary and seasoning to taste. Leave to marinate for 2 to 3 hours, turning from time to time.

Remove the fish from the marinade and cook under a moderate grill, or over medium coals on a barbecue, for about 6 minutes each side, basting frequently with the marinade during cooking. Serve on a bed of lettuce leaves, garnish with watercress and accompany with any remaining marinade. SERVES 4

Smoked Mackerel Gougère

Carol Bowen

350 g/12 oz smoked mackerel fillets, skinned
1 medium onion, sliced
150 g/5 oz butter
175 g/6 oz plain flour
300 ml/½ pint milk
3 tablespoons cider
2 tablespoons natural yogurt
salt and pepper
300 ml/½ pint water · 4 eggs, beaten
75 g/3 oz Cheddar cheese, grated
1 tablespoon dry breadcrumbs
chopped chives or parsley to garnish

Flake the mackerel. Fry the onion in 25 g/1 oz of the butter until golden. Stir in 25 g/1 oz of the flour, gradually add the milk and bring to the boil, stirring. Boil for 1 minute, then remove from the heat and mix in the cider, yogurt, flaked fish and seasoning.

Melt the remining butter in a saucepan with the water. Bring to the boil, take off the heat and beat in the remaining flour until just smooth. Gradually beat in the eggs, then the cheese.

Spoon the paste around the edge of a greased 1.15-litre/2-pint ovenproof dish. Spoon the fish sauce into the centre, sprinkle with the breadcrumbs and bake in a moderately hot oven (200 C, 400 F, gas 6) for 40 to 45 minutes. Serve garnished with chives or parsley. SERVES 4

Russian Salmon Pie

Carol Bowen

75 g/3 oz butter
1 small onion, finely chopped
100 g/4 oz button mushrooms, sliced
50 g/2 oz plain flour
300 ml/½ pint milk · salt and pepper
350 g/12 oz cooked salmon (fresh or canned),
flaked
1 hard-boiled egg, chopped
1 (368-g/13-oz) packet frozen puff pastry,
defrosted
beaten egg to glaze

Melt the butter in a saucepan and fry the onion in it for 5 minutes, until soft. Add the mushrooms and fry them for 2 to 3 minutes. Stir in the flour and cook for 1 minute, then gradually add the milk, bring to the boil and cook for 2 to 3 minutes, stirring. Season, mix in the fish and chopped egg and leave to cool.

Roll out the pastry thinly to give a 30-cm/12-in square. Pile the filling in the centre and brush the edges with beaten egg. Bring the two opposite corners of pastry to the centre of the filling and secure by pinching them together. Bring up the other two points and press these together to form an envelope shape. Press and secure the pastry edges together and flute the seams. Decorate the top with pastry leaves made from any pastry trimmings and glaze with the beaten egg.

Place on a dampened baking tray and cook in a hot oven (220 C, 425 F, gas 7) for 30 to 40 minutes, until crisp and golden. Serve hot or cold. SERVES 4

Coley Crumble

—— Carol Bowen ——

675 g/1½ lb coley fillet, skinned and cut into
bite-sized pieces
3 tablespoons oil
1 tablespoon vinegar
1 Spanish onion, chopped
salt and pepper
100 g/4 oz plain flour
50 g/2 oz butter or margarine
50 g/2 oz Cheddar cheese, grated
1 (425-g/15-oz) can peeled tomatoes, drained

Place the coley in a 1.15-litre/2-pint ovenproof dish. Mix
the oil, vinegar, onion and seasoning to taste, and pour
over the fish. Leave to marinate for 30 minutes.

Meanwhile sift the flour into a bowl, add a pinch of salt
and rub in the butter or margarine. Stir in the cheese.
Place the tomatoes on top of the fish and sprinkle with
the cheese crumble. Bake in a moderately hot oven (190 C,
375 F, gas 5) for 30 minutes or until golden. Serve
immediately. SERVES 4

Fish Boulangère

—— Carol Bowen ——

50 g/2 oz butter
1 clove garlic, crushed
675 g/1½ lb white fish fillets (cod, haddock or
plaice for example), skinned and cut into
bite-sized pieces
salt and pepper
1 large onion, sliced into rings
2 tablespoons chopped parsley
450 g/1 lb potatoes, par-cooked and thinly
sliced

Mix half the butter with the garlic and spread on the base
of a 1.15-litre/2-pint ovenproof dish. Cover with the
pieces of fish. Season lightly, top with the onion and
sprinkle with the parsley. Place the potato slices on top,
in an overlapping pattern. Dot with the remaining butter
and bake in a moderate oven (180 C, 350 F, gas 4) for
45 minutes, or until the potato topping is crisp and golden
and the fish is cooked. SERVES 4

Stuffed Plaice Florentine

Diana Jaggar

0.75–1 kg/1½–2 lb fresh spinach, cooked and
thoroughly drained
1 small onion, finely chopped
50 g/2 oz butter
2 egg yolks
a little grated nutmeg
salt and pepper
4 large fillets of plaice, skinned and trimmed
100 ml/4 fl oz dry white wine
juice of 1 lemon
25 g/1 oz plain flour
300 ml/½ pint milk
½ teaspoon French mustard
75 g/3 oz Cheddar cheese, grated
pinch of cayenne pepper
2 tablespoons single cream

Finely chop the spinach. Sauté the onion in half the
butter in a small saucepan, then add the spinach and
cook, stirring occasionally, for 5 minutes. Remove the
pan from the heat and add the egg yolks, nutmeg and salt
and pepper to taste. Cool.

Divide the spinach mixture between the plaice fillets
and roll them up from tail to head. Place in a greased
ovenproof dish, pour in the wine and lemon juice, and
cover the dish. Bake in a moderate oven (180c, 350f,
gas 4) for 20 minutes.

Meanwhile, melt the remaining butter in a small
saucepan, add the flour and stir for 1 minute. Pour in the
milk and bring to the boil, stirring continuously. Stir in
the mustard, most of the cheese, the cooking juices from
the fish, cayenne, salt, pepper and cream; heat gently
without boiling. Coat the fish rolls with this sauce and
sprinkle with the remaining cheese, then brown under a
hot grill. SERVES 4

Grilled Salmon Steaks

Elizabeth Pomeroy

4 fresh salmon steaks
salt and pepper
lemon juice to taste
50 g/2 oz butter, softened
GARNISH
lemon wedges
fresh dill leaves

Wash the salmon steaks to remove any blood. Dry them
on absorbent kitchen paper. Season with the salt, pepper
and lemon juice. Place on the grill rack and dot with
butter. Preheat the grill and cook the steaks for 8 to 10
minutes according to thickness. Turn the steaks over and
season the second side. Dot with butter and grill until the
flesh shrinks from the backbone.

Place the salmon steaks on a warmed serving plate and
garnish with lemon wedges and dill. Serve with Dill
Cream Sauce. SERVES 4

Dill Cream Sauce

Elizabeth Pomeroy

40 g/1½ oz butter
1 tablespoon finely chopped onion
40 g/1½ oz plain flour
300 ml/½ pint fish stock or milk
2 tablespoons chopped fresh dill *or*
1–2 teaspoons dill seeds
4 tablespoons soured cream
salt and pepper

Melt the butter and fry the onion until transparent.
Remove the pan from the heat and stir in the flour. Blend
in the stock or milk and bring to the boil. Add the dill and
simmer for 3 to 4 minutes, stirring steadily. Stir in the
soured cream and seasoning and serve.

Glazed Salmon Trout

Carol Bowen

75 g/3 oz butter
1 (2.25-kg/5-lb) salmon trout, cleaned
2 bay leaves
600 ml/1 pint liquid aspic jelly
a little cucumber skin, cut into matchstick
strips
a few small radishes, trimmed and thinly
sliced
1 teaspoon gelatine
2 tablespoons cold water
450 ml/$\frac{3}{4}$ pint mayonnaise
GARNISH (OPTIONAL)
watercress sprigs
cucumber slices
lemon slices

Line a large roasting tin with cooking foil and grease it with 25 g/1 oz of the butter.

Wash the fish well and tuck the bay leaves inside the body cavity. Arrange the fish in the tin on its stomach (rather than laying the fish on its side) and curling from opposite corners of the tin to give a curved shape. Dot the remaining butter over the fish. Bring the edges of the foil together, folding them over without letting the foil touch the fish. Cook in a moderate oven (160 C, 350 F, gas 3) for 1$\frac{1}{2}$ hours. Baste the fish with the juices in the tin during cooking. Remove from the oven, open out the foil and allow the fish to cool.

When cool, place the fish on a board and remove the skin, leaving the head and tail intact. Transfer to a serving dish and brush the fish with the liquid aspic. Arrange pieces of cucumber skin and radish slices along the side of the fish, dipping each piece into aspic before placing on the fish. Chill to set quickly.

Remove and discard any aspic jelly that has collected around the base of the fish. Spoon the remaining jelly over the fish and 'flood' the serving dish with a thin layer. Leave to set.

Sprinkle the gelatine on to the cold water in a small basin and place over a pan of simmering water until dissolved and clear. Stir this mixture into the mayonnaise and chill for about 15 minutes until thickened.

Place the mayonnaise in a piping bag fitted with a large star-shaped nozzle and pipe a decorative design along the backbone of the fish. Garnish with watercress sprigs, cucumber and lemon slices, if liked. Serve chilled, with a cucumber salad and new potatoes. SERVES 8 TO 10

Scallops au Gratin

Carol Bowen

12 scallops, cut into 2-cm/$\frac{3}{4}$-in pieces
150 ml/$\frac{1}{4}$ pint dry white wine
300 ml/$\frac{1}{2}$ pint water
salt and pepper
50 g/2 oz butter
1 medium onion, finely chopped
4 tablespoons plain flour
4 teaspoons chopped parsley
150 ml/$\frac{1}{4}$ pint single cream
675 g/1$\frac{1}{2}$ lb potatoes, boiled and mashed
50 g/2 oz fresh white breadcrumbs
75 g/3 oz Cheddar cheese, grated

Place the scallops in a saucepan with the wine, water and seasoning to taste. Bring to the boil, then simmer for about 10 minutes or until tender. Strain and reserve 400 ml/14 fl oz of the cooking liquor.

Melt the butter in a clean saucepan. Add the onion and cook for about 5 minutes, or until soft. Stir in the flour and cook for 1 minute. Gradually add the reserved liquor, stirring continuously, to make a smooth sauce. Bring to the boil and simmer for 2 minutes. Add the scallops, chopped parsley and cream. Adjust the seasoning and reheat gently but do not allow to boil.

Meanwhile, pipe or spoon the potato around the bases of four flameproof dishes. Brown under the grill until golden. Spoon the scallop mixture into the centres. Mix the breadcrumbs and cheese together and sprinkle over ths scallops. Lightly brown under a moderate grill and serve. SERVES 4

Poultry and Game

From inexpensive supper ideas to extravagant dinner party
dishes – they are all here. For example, there is an economical
Country Chicken and Mushroom Pie to delight your family
on a cold day, or an impressive Pheasant Vallée d'Auge
for more formal occasions.

Stir-fried Chicken, Duck with Black Cherry Sauce,
Deep-fried Chicken and Smoked Chicken in Lemon Mayonnaise

Deep-fried Chicken

(ILLUSTRATED ON PREVIOUS PAGE)

Select small chicken joints or drumsticks for deep frying. Remove the skin and trim off the wing ends. Coat the joints in well-seasoned flour and dip them in beaten egg. Cover the surface of the chicken completely with fine dry breadcrumbs, repeat the whole process and chill lightly before cooking.

Heat oil for deep frying to 180c/350f. Add the chicken pieces and cook until deep golden – if the chicken browns too quickly the flesh will not be cooked through, so do not allow the oil to become too hot. Drain on absorbent kitchen paper and arrange on a serving dish or napkin-lined basket. Garnish with wedges or slices of lemon and large deep-fried parsley sprigs (cook the sprigs until crisp and drain them on absorbent kitchen paper). Serve with a mixed salad.

Stir-fried Chicken

Bridget Jones

(ILLUSTRATED ON PREVIOUS PAGE)

350 g/12 oz uncooked boneless chicken meat
2 carrots
2 sticks celery
1 tablespoon shredded lemon rind
2 tablespoons oil
salt and pepper
100 g/4 oz button mushrooms, thinly sliced
25 g/1 oz flaked almonds
1 bunch spring onions, shredded lengthways

Cut the chicken meat into fine strips. Halve the carrots, slice them lengthways and cut the slices into fine strips. Cut the celery into thin strips of a similar length. Mix the carrots and celery with the lemon rind.

Heat the oil in a large frying pan and add the chicken and seasoning to taste. Stir-fry until the meat is lightly browned, then add the vegetable mixture and continue to cook for a few minutes. Stir in the mushrooms and cook for a few seconds. The cooked vegetables should be crisp. Transfer the stir-fry to serving bowls.

Quickly toss the almonds in the fat remaining in the pan until they are lightly browned, then stir in the spring onions. Spoon this mixture over the top of the chicken and serve immediately. SERVES 4

Duck with Black Cherry Sauce

Bridget Jones

(ILLUSTRATED ON PREVIOUS PAGE)

1 oven-ready duck (with giblets)
1 small onion, chopped
salt and pepper
1 tablespoon demerara sugar
1 (425-g/15-oz) can stoneless black cherries
1 tablespoon arrowroot
a little lemon juice
watercress to garnish

Place the duck giblets in a small saucepan and add cold water to cover. Add the onion and a little seasoning and bring to the boil, cover and simmer gently while the duck is cooking. Check that the stock does not reduce below the level of the giblets during cooking.

Place the duck on a roasting rack and stand it in a roasting tin. Prick the skin all over with a fork and sprinkle with seasoning and the sugar. Roast in a hot oven (220c, 425f, gas 7) for 20 minutes, then reduce the oven temperature to moderate (180c, 350f, gas 4) and cook for a further $1\frac{1}{4}$ hours. Baste the duck occasionally during cooking and cover the top with a piece of cooking foil if the skin browns too quickly.

Strain and reserve the giblet stock, boiling it down, if necessary, to give about 300 ml/$\frac{1}{2}$ pint. Cut the duck into four joints, arrange them on a serving dish and keep hot. Pour off all the fat from the roasting tin, reserving just the juices. Pour the stock into the tin with the syrup from the cherries and heat to boiling point. Blend the arrowroot with a little cold water and stir the mixture into the sauce. Bring back to the boil, stirring continuously, and simmer for 2 minutes. Taste and adjust the seasoning and sharpen with lemon juice to taste. Stir in the cherries and pour the sauce over the duck. Serve immediately, garnished with watercress. SERVES 4

Poule au Pot

Julia Roles

1 (1.5-kg/3½-lb) boiling chicken with giblets
600 ml/1 pint water
salt and pepper
3 onions, peeled
50 g/2 oz butter
6 carrots, thickly sliced
3 sticks celery, chopped
2 turnips, quartered
2 bay leaves
25 g/1 oz plain flour

Place the chicken giblets in a saucepan with the water and 1 teaspoon salt. Bring to the boil, then cover the pan, reduce the heat and simmer for 30 minutes.

Meanwhile, place an onion inside the chicken and truss as for a roasting chicken. Melt half the butter in a large flameproof casserole and brown the chicken all over; pour off the fat. Quarter the remaining onions and arrange round the chicken with the vegetables and bay leaves. Strain in the giblet stock and season with pepper. Cover and place in a moderate oven (160 c, 325 f, gas 3) for 2 to 2½ hours.

Arrange the cooked chicken and vegetables on a large serving platter and keep hot. Skim any fat off the sauce. Blend together the remaining butter and the flour to form a paste. Add to the sauce, a little at a time and stir over a gentle heat until thickened. Season the sauce and serve separately. SERVES 4 TO 6

Chicken Parisienne

Diana Jaggar

1 (1.5-kg/3½-lb) roasting chicken, boned
50 g/2 oz butter, softened
150 ml/¼ pint chicken stock
3 tablespoons sherry
STUFFING
1 onion, finely chopped
25 g/1 oz butter
225 g/8 oz each of veal and ham, minced
3 tablespoons fresh white breadcrumbs
2 teaspoons chopped parsley
1 teaspoon chopped tarragon
grated rind and juice of ½ lemon
1 egg, beaten

Open out the chicken and season well.

For the stuffing, fry the onion in the butter until soft. Cool, then mix with the meats, breadcrumbs, herbs and lemon rind. Bind with the lemon juice and egg, and add seasoning. Spread this stuffing in the bird and sew up.

Spread the 50 g/2 oz butter over the chicken, place in a roasting tin and pour in the stock and sherry. Cook in a moderately hot oven (190 c, 375 f, gas 5) for 1½ hours, basting well. Serve the chicken sliced. SERVES 4 TO 6

Poulet au Citron

Diana Jaggar

2 tablespoons oil · 50 g/2 oz butter
1 (1.5-kg/3½-lb) roasting chicken, jointed
1 onion, finely chopped
1 clove garlic, crushed
¼ teaspoon powdered saffron
250 ml/8 fl oz dry white wine
300 ml/½ pint chicken stock
pared rind and juice of 1 lemon
salt and pepper
175 g/6 oz button mushrooms, quartered
25 g/1 oz plain flour
2 egg yolks
150 ml/¼ pint single cream

Heat the oil in a large frying pan. Add half the butter and the chicken pieces and cook until browned all over. Transfer to a flameproof casserole. Add the onion and garlic to the fat remaining in the pan and cook until softened, then add the saffron, wine and stock. Bring to the boil, adding the lemon juice, salt and pepper, and pour over the chicken. Cover and simmer for 45 to 60 minutes. Cut the lemon rind into fine strips, blanch for a few minutes in boiling water and add most of the strips to the chicken at the end of the cooking time. Strain the cooking juices and keep the chicken hot.

For the sauce, melt the remaining butter in a saucepan, add the mushrooms and sauté them for a few minutes. Sprinkle in the flour and cook for 1 minute. Pour in the chicken juices and cook, stirring, until the sauce thickens. Pour some of this on to the yolks and cream, mix well and return to pan. Reheat gently without boiling, then spoon this sauce over the chicken and sprinkle with the reserve strips of lemon rind. SERVES 4

Chicken Cacciatore

Moya Maynard

4 chicken quarters · 75 g/3 oz butter
1 large onion, chopped
1 medium green pepper, deseeded and chopped
1 clove garlic, crushed
1 (396-g/14-oz) can peeled tomatoes
150 ml/¼ pint chicken stock
salt and pepper
watercress to garnish

Fry the chicken for 25 to 30 minutes in 50 g/2 oz of the butter, or until cooked through. Meanwhile, sauté the onion, green pepper and garlic in the remaining butter for about 10 minutes. Stir in the tomatoes, stock and seasoning. Cover and simmer for 15 minutes.

Spoon the sauce over the chicken on a heated serving dish. Garnish with watercress and serve with rice sprinkled with chopped parsley. SERVES 4

Chicken Provençal

—— Carol Bowen ——

4 tablespoons oil
4 chicken portions
2 onions, chopped
2 cloves garlic, crushed
2 green peppers, deseeded and finely diced
300 ml/½ pint dry white wine or stock
6 tomatoes, peeled and chopped
1 tablespoon tomato purée
bay leaf
1 teaspoon dried oregano
salt and pepper

Heat the oil in a flameproof casserole, add the chicken and fry it on all sides until golden. Remove with a slotted spoon and add the onions, garlic and peppers. Cook for about 5 minutes to soften, then drain away any excess oil.

Return the chicken to the casserole. Add the wine, tomatoes, tomato purée, bay leaf and oregano. Season generously, then cover the casserole and simmer it for 1¼ hours.

Remove the bay leaf and taste and adjust the seasoning if necessary before serving with saffron rice. SERVES 4

Salami-stuffed Chicken

—— Carol Bowen ——

1 (1.4-kg/3-lb) oven-ready chicken, boned
1 (170-g/6-oz) packet Brussels liver pâté
50 g/2 oz fresh brown breadcrumbs
25 g/1 oz chopped mixed nuts
2 tablespoons chopped parsley
2 tablespoons chopped chives
pinch of grated nutmeg
salt and pepper
1–2 tablespoons milk
100 g/4 oz salami, sliced
2 knackwurst
25 g/1 oz butter
parsley sprigs to garnish

Place the chicken, skin side down, on a large board. Throughly mix the pâté, breadcrumbs, nuts, parsley, chives, nutmeg and seasoning, softening with the milk if necessary. Spread one third of this pâté mixture over the chicken and arrange the salami on top. Spread another third of the pâté on top and cover with the knackwurst, end to end. Top with the final third of pâté.

Sew up the chicken with fine thread to give a good shape, enclosing the stuffing, and weigh the bird. Season and dot with the butter. Place in a roasting tin and cook in a moderately hot oven (190 C, 375 F, gas 5), allowing 25 minutes per 450 g/1 lb, basting from time to time.

When cooked allow to cool, remove the thread and chill. Serve sliced, garnished with parsley, with new potatoes and a mixed salad. SERVES 6 TO 8

Poulet aux Amandes

— Diana Jaggar —

100 g/4 oz butter
1 (1.5-kg/3½-lb) roasting chicken, prepared
tarragon sprig
150 ml/¼ pint white wine or chicken stock
50 g/2 oz almonds, blanched and shredded
225 g/8 oz red peppers, deseeded and sliced
1 onion, chopped
20 g/¾ oz plain flour
300 ml/½ pint chicken stock
pinch of mace
salt and pepper
150 ml/¼ pint single cream

Put 15 g/½ oz of the butter inside the bird with the tarragon; spread 40 g/1½ oz of the butter over the top. Place in a roasting tin with the wine or stock. Roast in a moderately hot oven (200 C, 400 F, gas 6) for 1–1¼ hours.
   Fry the almonds in the remaining butter until brown. Add the vegetables and sauté until soft. Remove, then add the flour. Cook for 1 minute, then stir in the stock, mace, seasoning, almond and pepper mixture, and strained chicken juices. Boil, reduce the heat and add the cream, then heat gently. Joint the chicken and arrange it on a dish with the sauce. SERVES 4 TO 6

Coq au Vin

— Julia Roles —

1 (2-kg/4½-lb) chicken with giblets, jointed
salt and pepper
100 g/4 oz bacon, chopped
20 button onions, peeled
75 g/3 oz butter
4 tablespoons brandy
450 ml/¾ pint red wine
225 g/8 oz mushrooms, sliced
2 cloves garlic, crushed
2 teaspoons soft brown sugar
bouquet garni
pinch of grated nutmeg
40 g/1½ oz plain flour
chopped parsley to garnish

Simmer the giblets for 30 minutes in salted water to cover. Sauté the bacon and onions in half the butter, in a flameproof casserole, until golden. Remove and brown the chicken in the fat. Add the brandy and ignite. Return the bacon and onions and add the wine, 150 ml/¼ pint of the strained giblet stock, the mushrooms, garlic, sugar, bouquet garni, nutmeg and pepper. Boil, then cover and cook in a moderate oven (180 C, 350 F, gas 4) for 1 hour.
   Remove the chicken and keep hot. Blend the remaining butter and flour, and gradually whisk into the sauce. Heat until thickened. Replace the chicken and sprinkle with parsley. SERVES 4

Poussin a l'Estragon

Diana Jaggar

1 lemon
handful of fresh tarragon
3 (675–900-g/1½–2-lb) poussins, prepared
175 g/6 oz butter
250 ml/8 fl oz white wine
225 g/8 oz onions, finely chopped
225 g/8 oz button mushrooms, sliced
40 g/1½ oz plain flour
300 ml/½ pint chicken stock
1 tablespoon chopped parsley
salt and pepper

Squeeze and reserve the juice from the lemon. Remove, chop and reserve the leaves from the fresh tarragon. Cut up the lemon skin and put a piece inside each bird with the tarragon stalks and a knob of butter. Keep 50 g/2 oz of the butter and spread the remainder over the poussins. Put them in a roasting tin, pour over the wine and cook in a moderate oven (180 c, 350 f, gas 4) for 40 to 50 minutes.

Melt the reserved butter in a small saucepan. Add the onions and cook until soft, then add the mushrooms and sauté for a few minutes. Sprinkle the flour into the pan and cook for 1 minute. Gradually stir in the stock, bring to the boil and add the lemon juice, tarragon, parsley and seasoning. Bring to the boil and simmer for 15 minutes.

When the poussins are cooked, strain the juices from the roasting tin into the sauce and cook until thickened to a coating consistency. Just before serving, cut each bird in half (poultry scissors are best for this) and arrange on a heated serving dish. Spoon over the sauce and serve with sautéd button mushrooms. SERVES 6

Chicken with Pineapple

Julia Roles

4 chicken joints
4 tablespoons olive oil
1 green pepper, deseeded and chopped
2 sticks celery, chopped
1 onion, chopped
1 (198-g/7-oz) can pineapple slices
1 tablespoon each of soy sauce, lemon juice
and tomato purée
salt and pepper

Fry the chicken in the oil until golden. Transfer to a casserole. Add the vegetables to the pan and sauté until softened. Transfer to the casserole with the pineapple syrup, soy sauce, lemon juice, tomato purée and seasoning. Cover and cook in a moderate oven (180 c, 350 f, gas 4) for 45 minutes. Arrange the halved pineapple slices on top of the chicken and return, uncovered, to the oven for a final 15 minutes. Serve with rice and mushrooms. SERVES 4

Roast Tarragon Chicken

Elizabeth Pomeroy

1 (1.5-kg/3½-lb) roasting chicken
50 g/2 oz butter
2 tablespoons chopped fresh tarragon *or*
2 teaspoons dried tarragon
1 small clove garlic
salt and pepper
300 ml/½ pint giblet stock
2 tablespoons brandy or sherry
4 tablespoons double cream

Truss the chicken neatly. Cream together the butter and tarragon. Crush the garlic and blend it into the butter. Season to taste with salt and pepper. Spread some of the tarragon butter over the bird and put the rest inside.

Place the bird on its side on a rack in the roasting pan. Pour in the stock and cook in a moderately hot oven (200 C, 400 F, gas 6) for 20 minutes. Turn the bird on to the other side, baste and roast for another 20 minutes. Turn the chicken breast upwards and baste again. Continue roasting for a further 20 minutes or until the juice runs amber-coloured when the thigh is pierced with a skewer.

Place the chicken on a heated serving dish and keep warm. Remove the rack from the roasting pan. Pour off the fat, retaining the juices. Add the brandy or sherry, boil, then stir in the cream. Season and pour into a warmed sauce boat. SERVES 4

Pot-roasted Chicken

Elizabeth Pomeroy

1 (1.25-kg/2½-lb) chicken, dressed
40 g/1½ oz butter, softened
1 tablespoon chopped fresh tarragon
1 small clove garlic, crushed
salt and pepper
olive oil for basting
6 or 8 button onions, peeled
1 stick celery, chopped
100 ml/4 fl oz white wine
3–4 tablespoons soured cream
GIBLET STOCK
chicken giblets
bouquet garni
6 black peppercorns
GARNISH
fresh tarragon leaves

Truss the chicken neatly. Cream together the butter, chopped tarragon, garlic and seasoning. Put this herb butter inside the chicken and brush the chicken liberally with olive oil. Heat a tablespoon of oil in a deep flameproof casserole and brown the chicken over a brisk heat. Add the onions and celery, season with salt and pepper, then add the wine. Simmer for a minute, lower the heat, cover and cook very gently for 45 minutes, turning the chicken from time to time.

Meanwhile, clean the giblets, place in a saucepan with cold water to cover and add the bouquet garni, salt and peppercorns. Cover and simmer gently until required.

Pierce the leg of the chicken. If the juice runs amber coloured, the chicken is cooked; if it runs red, continue cooking gently until done. Add a little giblet stock to the casserole if the liquid has evaporated.

When the chicken is cooked, remove from the casserole, tipping it so that the juices inside run out into the pot. Add a cupful of the giblet stock; boil briskly to reduce. Mix the soured cream with 3 to 4 tablespoons of the chicken gravy, pour this into the casserole and heat through. Adjust the seasoning.

Replace the chicken in the casserole and garnish with fresh tarragon leaves, or serve the chicken on a platter and hand the sauce separately. SERVES 4

Chicken and Ham Pie à la Russe

Elizabeth Pomeroy

100–150 g/4–5 oz cooked chicken, chopped
50 g/2 oz cooked ham, diced
150 g/5 oz Cheddar cheese, diced
50 g/2 oz mushrooms, chopped
1 tablespoon chopped parsley
salt and pepper
1 egg, beaten
225 g/8 oz frozen puff pastry, defrosted
beaten egg to glaze

Mix together the chicken, ham, cheese, mushrooms and parsley. Season to taste, then stir the egg into the mixture. Roll the pastry thinly into a rectangle 39 × 26 cm/ 15 × 10 in and pile the filling in the centre. Fold the corners of the square to the centre and seal the edges with beaten egg. Glaze the pie evenly all over with egg. Use any remaining pastry to make decorations and a tassel, glaze with egg and arrange on the pie. Open the outer corners of the envelope slightly to allow steam to escape during cooking.

Bake in a hot oven (220 C, 425 F, gas 7) for 25 minutes until well risen and golden brown. Serve hot with tomato quarters and fresh watercress. SERVES 4 TO 6

Chicken and Ham Turnovers

Carol Bowen

40 g/1½ oz butter or margarine
1 medium onion, chopped
50 g/2 oz mushrooms, coarsely chopped
40 g/1½ oz plain flour
300 ml/½ pint milk
1 teaspoon French mustard
salt and pepper
175 g/6 oz cooked chicken meat, coarsely chopped
100 g/4 oz cooked ham, cubed
1 (368-g/13-oz) packet frozen puff pastry, defrosted
beaten egg to glaze

Melt the butter or margarine in a small saucepan. Add the onion and mushrooms and cook gently for 2 minutes until beginning to soften. Stir in the flour and cook for 1minute. Gradually add the milk to make a sauce. Bring to the boil, stirring, then reduce the heat and cook for 2 minutes. Remove from the heat, add the mustard, seasoning to taste, chicken and ham. Leave to cool.

Roll out the pastry on a lightly floured surface to a 30 × 45-cm/12 × 18-in rectangle and cut into six 15-cm/6-in squares. Divide the chicken mixture into six portions. Pile on to the pastry squares, brush the edges with beaten egg and press together over the filling, sealing the edges well, to form triangles. Cut two slits in the tops of the turnovers to allow any steam to escape. Use any pastry trimmings to decorate the turnovers. Glaze with beaten egg, place on a dampened baking tray and bake in a hot oven (220 c, 425 f, gas 7) for 25 to 35 minutes until golden brown and cooked through. Serve with a crisp salad. MAKES 6

Devilled Chicken Legs

Carol Bowen

about 100 ml/4 fl oz dry sherry
1 tablespoon tarragon vinegar
2 teaspoons Worcestershire sauce
2 teaspoons prepared English mustard
salt and pepper
4 chicken leg joints *or* 8 chicken drumsticks
oil for basting

Mix the sherry, vinegar, Worcestershire sauce, mustard and seasoning to taste in a small bowl. Make a few neat cuts in the chicken flesh and place in a shallow dish. Pour the sherry mixture on top and leave the chicken to marinate for at least 1 hour, turning from time to time in the mixture.

Cook the chicken under a moderate grill or on a barbecue over medium coals for 10 to 15 minutes on each side, depending upon size, basting alternately with the sherry mixture and oil. Serve hot, with salad ingredients and pickle. SERVES 4

Country Chicken and Mushroom Pie

— Elizabeth Pomeroy —

1 small boiling chicken
1 medium onion, chopped
1 stick celery, chopped
1–2 carrots, sliced
bay leaf
1 parsley sprig
thyme or rosemary sprig
salt and pepper
50 g/2 oz belly of pork, pickled or smoked
75 g/3 oz mushrooms, sliced
1 (368-g/13-oz) packet frozen puff pastry, defrosted
beaten egg to glaze
SAUCE
50 g/2 oz butter or margarine
40 g/1½ oz plain flour
150 ml/¼ pint milk
1 teaspoon lemon juice
2 tablespoons chopped parsley

Boil the bird in enough water to cover with the onion, celery, carrots, bay leaf, parsley, thyme or rosemary and seasoning. This will take about 1½ hours. When the bird is cooked, lift it from the pan, remove the flesh and cut it into neat pieces. Strain the stock and skim off the fat.

Dice the belly of pork and mix it with the chicken meat. Then make the sauce: melt the butter or margarine in a saucepan, stir in the flour and remove the pan from the heat. Gradually add the milk, stirring continuously. Still stirring, bring to simmering point, then stir in 150 ml/¼ pint of the reserved stock. Season with lemon juice, salt and pepper, and stir in the parsley. Mix in the chicken and turn into a deep oval pie dish with a pie funnel in the centre. Cover with the sliced mushrooms. Allow to become quite cold.

Roll out the pastry to 5 mm/¼ in thick, dampen the rim of the dish and cover with a strip of pastry cut from the outside of the whole piece. Brush the pastry strip with water and cover with the remaining pastry. Press the edges together and trim off the surplus. Knock up and flute the edges. Cut two slits for the steam to escape and make a hole into the pie funnel with a skewer. Brush the top with beaten egg and decorate with any pastry trimmings made into leaves. Glaze the decorations and bake the pie in a hot oven (230 c, 450 f, gas 8) for 20 minutes. Reduce to moderately hot (190 c, 375 f, gas 5) for a further 20 minutes or until the pastry is completely cooked. SERVES 4

Chicken Kiev

— Elizabeth Pomeroy —

2 (1.5-kg/3-lb) roasting chickens
100 g/4 oz unsalted butter, softened
grated rind and juice of 1 lemon
4 teaspoons chopped parsley
1 teaspoon chopped tarragon or rosemary
pinch of grated nutmeg or mace
salt and pepper
a little seasoned flour · 1 egg, beaten
fine fresh breadcrumbs for coating
oil for deep frying

Carefully fillet the two sides of the breast of each chicken, leaving the wing bones joined to them. Beat flat.

Cream together the butter, lemon rind and herbs, and flavour to taste with lemon juice, spice and seasoning. Shape into a rectangle and chill until hard. Cut the block of butter into four pieces, lay one on each chicken breast, then fold up neatly, pressing together well. Secure with wooden cocktail sticks. Roll in seasoned flour and pat off any surplus. Coat with beaten egg and the breadcrumbs. Coat a second time with egg and crumbs for a perfect finish. Chill thoroughly before frying.

Heat the fat for deep frying to 190–195 c/375–380 f. Put the chicken into the greased frying basket and cook in the hot oil until golden brown. Drain on absorbent kitchen paper, remove the cocktail sticks and put a cutlet frill on each wing bone. Serve immediately. SERVES 4

Smoked Chicken in Lemon Mayonnaise

— Carol Bowen —

1 (1.75-kg/4-lb) smoked chicken
1 small fresh pineapple
juice of 1 lemon
300 ml/½ pint mayonnaise
salt and pepper
25 g/1 oz walnuts, chopped
GARNISH
watercress sprigs

Remove the meat from the chicken. Slice the white meat and cut the dark wing and leg meat into bite-sized pieces.

Slice the pineapple, removing the skin and centre core. Halve three slices and reserve them for the garnish. Chop the remaining pineapple into bite-sized pieces.

Stir the lemon juice into the mayonnaise and season to taste. Mix about 4 tablespoons of the mayonnaise with the dark meat and arrange on a serving dish. Cover with the chopped pineapple. Lay the slices of white meat on top and coat with the remaining mayonnaise. Sprinkle with the chopped walnuts and garnish the dish with watercress and the reserved halved slices of pineapple. SERVES 4 TO 6

Chicken Croquettes with Almonds

— Audrey Ellis —

2 chicken wing portions
300 ml/½ pint chicken stock
40 g/1½ oz flaked almonds
50 g/2 oz butter
1 tablespoon plain flour
4 tablespoons milk
2 eggs · ¼ teaspoon mace
salt and pepper
seasoned flour
toasted breadcrumbs
oil for frying
50 g/2 oz whole almonds, blanched

Place the chicken portions in a saucepan with the stock. Cover and cook gently for 40 minutes, until tender, then leave to cool in the stock. Remove the chicken, reserving the stock. Strip all the flesh from the joints and mince it with the flaked almonds.

Melt 15 g/½ oz of the butter in a saucepan and stir in the flour. Gradually stir in the milk and 3 or 4 tablespoons of the stock, then bring to the boil. Off the heat, blend in 1 egg yolk, the mace and seasoning. Add the minced chicken and mix well. Chill.

Shape the chicken mixture into twelve croquettes. Beat the remaining egg white with the egg. Coat the croquettes in seasoned flour, then in the beaten egg and egg white, and finally toss them in the breadcrumbs. Fry the croquettes, four at a time, in deep hot oil for about 5 minutes, until crisp and golden brown. Drain well on absorbent kitchen paper. Fry the almonds in the remaining butter and serve with a mixed salad. SERVES 4

Moroccan Jellied Chicken

— Audrey Ellis —

1 (1.5-kg/3½-lb) chicken
2 tablespoons corn oil
2 tablespoons lemon juice
½ teaspoon turmeric
½ teaspoon ground cardamom
1 teaspoon salt
¼ teaspoon pepper
100 ml/4 fl oz water

Skin the chicken. Combine the oil, lemon juice, turmeric, cardamom, salt and pepper in a flameproof casserole. Pour in the water and stir well. Bring to the boil, then place the chicken in the casserole, cover tightly and simmer carefully for about 1 hour, or until the chicken is tender. Remove the lid to turn the chicken every 25 minutes, and add a little more water if necessary.

Remove the chicken from the pan, spoon over the sauce and allow to cool. The sauce will set to give a golden jelly. Serve with an orange salad. SERVES 4 TO 6

Polish Paprika Chicken

— Audrey Ellis —

1 clove garlic, finely crushed
$\frac{1}{4}$ teaspoon dried basil
pinch of ground cloves
1 tablespoon paprika
$\frac{1}{4}$ teaspoon mace
40 g/1$\frac{1}{2}$ oz seasoned plain flour
4 chicken portions
1 tablespoon oil
25 g/1 oz butter
1 (70-g/2$\frac{3}{4}$-oz) can pimentos
4 tablespoons dry sherry
1 tablespoon tomato purée
1 teaspoon sugar
1 tablespoon chopped parsley
150 ml/$\frac{1}{4}$ pint soured cream

Add the garlic, basil and spices to the seasoned flour. Use to coat the chicken portions. Heat the oil and butter in a flameproof casserole and brown the chicken on all sides. Drain the pimentos, reserving the juice, finely chop and add to the casserole. Combine the liquid from the can with the sherry, tomato purée and sugar and pour over the chicken. Cover and cook in a moderate oven (180 C, 350 F, gas 4) for about 1 hour, or until tender. Mix the parsley with the soured cream, spoon over the chicken and return to the oven for a further 10 minutes. SERVES 4.

Sunshine Chicken

— Audrey Ellis —

2 tablespoons oil
4 chicken portions
1 large onion, sliced
2 rindless rashers bacon, chopped
50 g/2 oz mushrooms, sliced
finely grated rind and juice of 1 orange
1 (326-g/11$\frac{1}{2}$-oz) can sweet corn with peppers
salt and pepper

Heat the oil, add the chicken portions and cook until brown on all sides. Remove and drain well.

Add the onion and bacon to the pan and fry gently until golden brown. Add the mushrooms and fry for a further 2 minutes. Stir in the orange rind and juice and the sweet corn with the liquid from the can. Season well and bring to the boil.

Spoon the corn mixture into an ovenproof dish and place the chicken portions on top. Cover with foil or a lid and cook in a moderately hot oven (190 C, 375 F, gas 5) for about 1 hour, or until the chicken is tender. SERVES 4

Stir-fried Turkey with Celery

———— Audrey Ellis ————

450 g/1 lb boneless uncooked turkey
5 sticks celery
2 tablespoons oil
75 g/3 oz mushrooms, sliced
1 tablespoon soy sauce
salt and pepper
1 tablespoon cornflour
4 tablespoons chicken stock
chopped parsley to garnish

Cut the turkey into slices. String the celery and cut it into short lengths.

Heat the oil in a large frying pan and use to fry the turkey slices briskly for about 5 minutes, stirring all the time. Add the celery, mushrooms and soy sauce and season with a little salt and pepper. Cook the mixture for a further 5 minutes, stirring frequently.

Blend the cornflour with the stock, add to the mixture in the frying pan and bring to the boil, stirring continuously. Simmer for 2 minutes before serving sprinkled with chopped parsley. SERVES 4

Turkey with Red Dawn Sauce

———— Audrey Ellis ————

2 teaspoons oil
10 tablespoons water
2 tablespoons vinegar
2 teaspoons brown sugar
salt
2 teaspoons cornflour
450 g/1 lb cooked turkey, diced
2 teaspoons tomato purée
2 teaspoons soy sauce
175 g/6 oz carrot, grated

Heat the oil and half the water, then carefully add the vinegar, sugar and salt to taste. Bring to the boil.

Mix the cornflour with the rest of the water and blend into the sauce. Bring back to the boil, stirring constantly, and cook for 2 to 3 minutes.

Add the cooked turkey, tomato purée, soy sauce and grated carrot and reheat carefully to boiling point. Simmer for 5 minutes. SERVES 4

Pheasant Vallée d'Auge

Diana Jaggar

1 tablespoon oil
50 g/2 oz butter
1 plump oven-ready pheasant
100 ml/4 fl oz Calvados
1 onion, thinly sliced
2 sticks celery, thinly sliced
225 g/8 oz Cox's apples, peeled and sliced
15 g/½ oz plain flour
100 ml/4 fl oz white wine
300 ml/½ pint chicken stock
salt and pepper
150 ml/¼ pint double cream

Heat the oil and 25 g/1 oz of the butter in a frying pan and cook the bird, turning occasionally, until browned. Add and ignite the Calvados. Transfer the pheasant to a flameproof casserole. Sauté the onion in the remaining butter for 5 minutes. Add the celery and apple, cook for 5 minutes, then stir in the flour, wine and stock. Bring to the boil, stirring, season and pour over the pheasant. Cover and simmer for 45 to 50 minutes.

Lift the pheasant on to a serving dish and keep it hot. Liquidise or sieve the sauce, skimmed of fat, bring to the boil, whisk in the cream and heat without boiling. Season and serve with the pheasant. SERVES 4 TO 6

Pheasant Casserole with Chestnuts

Diana Jaggar

1 tablespoon oil
25 g/1 oz butter
1 plump oven-ready pheasant
225 g/8 oz button onions, peeled
225 g/8 oz fresh chestnuts, peeled
25 g/1 oz plain flour
450 g/¾ pint chicken stock
100 ml/4 fl oz red wine
grated rind and juice of 1 orange
2 teaspoons redcurrant jelly
bay leaf
salt and pepper

Heat the oil and butter in a frying pan and brown the bird. Cut it into portions and place in an ovenproof casserole. Cook the onions and chestnuts in the pan until golden, then transfer to the casserole. Put the flour in the pan and cook for 1 minute before whisking in the stock, wine, orange rind and juice, and the redcurrant jelly. Bring to the boil, stirring, and add the bay leaf and seasoning. Pour the sauce over the pheasant, cover and cook in a moderate oven (160 C, 325 F, gas 3) for 1½–2 hours. Remove the bay leaf, skim off any fat and adjust the seasoning. SERVES 4 TO 6

Partridge Bourguignonne

Diana Jaggar

2 oven-ready partridges
50 g/2 oz butter
175 g/6 oz rindless lean bacon, cut into strips
150 ml/$\frac{1}{4}$ pint red wine
300 ml/$\frac{1}{2}$ pint chicken stock
1 teaspoon tomato purée
bouquet garni
salt and pepper
350 g/12 oz pickling onions, peeled
1 clove garlic, crushed
175 g/6 oz button mushrooms
1 tablespoon chopped parsley

Brown the birds in 25 g/1 oz of the butter. Transfer to an ovenproof casserole. Brown the bacon, add the wine, stock and tomato purée; boil. Pour into the casserole, adding the bouquet garni and seasoning. Cover and cook in a moderate oven (180c, 350f, gas 4) for 30 minutes.

Brown the onions and garlic in the remaining butter. Stir in the mushrooms, add the mixture to the casserole with the parsley and cook for a further 30 minutes.

Cut each bird in half, remove the backbone and trim the bones; place in a serving dish. Season the sauce and spoon over the birds. SERVES 4

Casseroled Grouse

Julia Roles

4 mature grouse, trussed
salt and pepper
25 g/1 oz butter
2 tablespoons olive oil
6 shallots, roughly chopped
2 sticks celery, chopped
2 cloves garlic, crushed
1–2 tablespoons plain flour
300 ml/$\frac{1}{2}$ pint beef stock
300 ml/$\frac{1}{2}$ pint red wine
8 juniper berries, crushed
2 teaspoons chopped fresh marjoram *or*
1 teaspoon dried marjoram
225 g/8 oz button mushrooms

Season the grouse and brown them in the butter and oil in a flameproof casserole. Remove the birds from the casserole. Sauté the shallots, celery and garlic in the remaining fat, then add the flour. Brown lightly, then blend in the stock and wine, and boil, stirring constantly.

Replace the grouse and stir in the juniper berries and marjoram. Season, cover and cook in a moderate oven (180c, 350f, gas 4) for 1 hour. Add the mushrooms and cook for 30 minutes. SERVES 4

Guinea Chick with Cream, Rosemary and Brandy Sauce

Elizabeth Pomeroy

1 guinea chick
rosemary sprig
bay leaf
600 ml/1 pint water
1 chicken stock cube
65 g/2½ oz butter
1 medium onion, chopped
100 g/4 oz button mushrooms
4 tablespoons brandy
2 teaspoons plain flour
150 ml/¼ pint single cream
1 teaspoon finely chopped fresh rosemary *or*
½ teaspoon dried rosemary
GARNISH
lemon slices
rosemary sprigs

Cut the guinea chick in half down the backbone. Put the giblets in a saucepan with the rosemary sprig, bay leaf and water. Crumble in the stock cube, cover and simmer until required.

Melt 50 g/2 oz of the butter in a flameproof casserole, add the onion and mushrooms and fry gently until softened. Put the bird in the casserole and fry briskly until golden brown all over. Warm and ignite half the brandy, pour over the bird and shake the casserole. Add the strained giblet stock, bring to the boil, cover and simmer gently on top of the cooker or in a moderate oven (160 C, 325 F, gas 3) for 45 to 60 minutes or until tender. Remove the guinea chick.

Cream the remaining butter and flour together. Divide into little pieces and whisk them into the cooking liquid. Cook gently, stirring, until thickened to a sauce. Mix the cream, remaining brandy and a little of the sauce and blend this back into the casserole. Season and add the chopped rosemary. Replace the bird, heat without boiling and serve, garnished with lemon slices and rosemary sprigs. SERVES 2

Pork and Apricot Kebabs

Bridget Jones

(ILLUSTRATED ON PREVIOUS PAGE)

450 g/1 lb lean boneless pork
1 (410-g/14½-oz) can apricot halves
2 green peppers, deseeded
16 bay leaves
salt and pepper
1 tablespoon chopped rosemary
2 tablespoons oil
1 teaspoon prepared mustard

Cut the pork into neat cubes. Drain the apricot halves and reserve the juice. Cut the peppers into eighths. Thread the meat, apricots, peppers and bay leaves on to eight metal skewers.

Mix the syrup from the fruit with seasoning to taste, the rosemary, oil and mustard and brush the kebabs generously with this mixture. Cook under a hot grill, turning the skewers frequently, until the meat is well browned and cooked through. Brush frequently with the liquid mixture during cooking.

Heat the remaining liquid in a small saucepan and boil rapidly to reduce to a small amount of glaze. Pour this over the kebabs and serve them on a salad or on a bed of cooked rice. SERVES 4

Beef and Walnut Cobbler

Jill Spencer

675 g/1½ lb chuck steak, cubed
250 g/9 oz plain flour
salt and pepper
100 g/4 oz margarine
2 onions, sliced
1 green pepper, deseeded and sliced
1 clove garlic, crushed
450 ml/¾ pint beef stock
2 tablespoons tomato purée
½ teaspoon bicarbonate of soda
1 teaspoon cream of tartar
1 egg, beaten
5 tablespoons milk
25 g/1 oz walnuts, chopped

Toss the meat in 25 g/1 oz of the flour and plenty of seasoning. Melt half the margarine in a flameproof casserole and sauté the vegetables and garlic in it for 5 minutes. Remove and reserve the vegetables, then add the meat and cook until browned. Replace the vegetables, add seasoning, stock and the tomato purée. Cover and

cook in a moderately hot oven (190 C, 375 F, gas 5) for 1½ hours.

Place the remaining flour and margarine, a pinch of salt, the bicarbonate of soda, cream of tartar, egg and milk in the bowl of a food mixer and switch on to a slow speed to make a soft dough. Knead lightly, roll out and cut out 5 cm/2 in circles. Place these overlapping, on top of the meat, glaze with a little egg or milk and sprinkle with the walnuts. Return to a hot oven (220 C, 425 F, gas 7) for 20 to 25 minutes. Garnish with parsley before serving. SERVES 4 TO 6

Orange-glazed Cutlets

Bridget Jones

(ILLUSTRATED ON PREVIOUS PAGE)

8 lamb cutlets
grated rind and juice of 1 large orange
2 tablespoons oil
1 clove garlic, crushed
salt and pepper
dash of Worcestershire sauce
1 tablespoon demerara sugar
GARNISH
orange slices
watercress

Trim any excess fat off the cutlets and place them in a foil-lined grill pan. Mix the orange rind and juice with the oil, garlic, seasoning, Worcestershire sauce and sugar. Brush the lamb generously with this mixture and cook under a hot grill, brushing frequently with the glaze, until browned on top. Turn the cutlets, glaze them and cook until the second side is browned and the meat is cooked to taste.

Arrange the cutlets on a heated serving dish and serve immediately, garnished with whole or halved orange slices and watercress. SERVES 4

Beef Wellington

Diana Jaggar

1.25 kg/2½ lb whole fillet of beef, trimmed
2 tablespoons brandy
1 clove garlic, cut in half
salt and pepper
50 g/2 oz butter
225 g/8 oz onions, finely chopped
225 g/8 oz mushrooms, finely chopped
3 sliced cooked ham, cut in half
1 (368-g/13-oz) packet frozen puff pastry,
defrosted
beaten egg to glaze

Marinate the fillet in the brandy for a few hours. Rub the meat with the garlic and season with pepper. Brown the fillet all over in the butter, cover with the brandy marinade and ignite. Remove the beef and cool. Add the onions and mushrooms to the fat and fry until soft. Season and cool. Cut the fillet two-thirds through into six portions. Sandwich the folded ham into the cuts.

Roll the pastry out to a large rectangle. Spread with the mushroom mixture and lay the fillet on top, cut side down. Make into a neat parcel and seal the edges.

Place a piece of greased greaseproof paper on a baking tray. Lift the beef on to the tray with the folds underneath. Glaze and score the pastry. Use any pastry trimmings to make leaves. Bake in a hot oven (230 c, 450 f, gas 8) for 30 to 40 minutes until browned. SERVES 6

Sweet and Sour Meatballs

Moya Maynard

225 g/8 oz minced beef
225 g/8 oz sausagemeat
50 g/2 oz onion, grated
½ teaspoon dried mixed herbs
salt and pepper
2 tablespoons oil
1 carrot, peeled and cut into small strips
450 ml/¾ pint beef stock
4 tablespoons malt vinegar
75 g/3 oz demerara sugar
4 teaspoons cornflour
1 teaspoon soy sauce

Mix the first five ingredients, then form into 18 to 20 balls. Fry in the oil for 15 to 20 minutes and drain. Cook the carrot, stock, vinegar and sugar in a saucepan for 5 minutes. Blend the cornflour with the soy sauce and a little water, stir in some of the hot liquid, return to the pan and boil, stirring. Serve the meatballs on noodles and pour the sauce on top. SERVES 4

Hungarian Goulash

Julia Roles

3 tablespoons oil
0.75–1 kg/1½–2 lb skirt steak, cubed
3 onions, sliced
1 red pepper, deseeded and chopped
25 g/1 oz plain flour
2 tablespoons paprika
450 g/1 lb tomatoes, peeled and chopped
600 ml/1 pint beef stock
bouquet garni
1 teaspoon dried thyme
salt
150 ml/¼ pint soured cream
parsley sprigs to garnish

Heat the oil in a flameproof casserole, add the meat and cook until browned all over, then remove from the pan.

Lower the heat and sauté the onions and red pepper in the fat remaining in the casserole. When they are softened sprinkle in the flour and paprika, then cook, stirring, for 1 minute. Add the tomatoes and stock and bring to simmering point, stirring continuously. Return the meat to the casserole, add the bouquet garni and thyme and season with salt. Cover the casserole and place in a moderate oven (160 C, 325 F, gas 3) for 2½ to 3 hours.

Remove the bouquet garni from the goulash before serving. Spoon a little of the soured cream on top of the goulash and garnish with the parsley. Serve the remaining soured cream separately. SERVES 4

Beef Brazilian Style

Julia Roles

1 kg/2 lb skirt steak, cut in strips
3 tablespoons oil
3 onions, sliced into rings
1 clove garlic, crushed
25 g/1 oz plain flour
150 ml/¼ pint black coffee
150 ml/¼ pint beef stock or red wine
1 (396-g/14-oz) can peeled tomatoes
salt and pepper
pinch of grated nutmeg
2 teaspoons soft brown sugar

Fry the meat in the oil, lower the heat, add the onions and garlic and cook until soft. Stir in the flour and cook for 1 minute. Gradually mix in the coffee and stock or wine, then add the tomatoes. Season, add the nutmeg and soft brown sugar, bring to simmering point and transfer to an ovenproof casserole. Cook, covered, in a moderate oven (160 C, 325 F, gas 3) for 2 hours. SERVES 4

Boeuf à la Provençale

— Julia Roles —

1 kg/2 lb lean braising or stewing steak
3 tablespoons olive oil
175 g/6 oz rindless streaky bacon, chopped
225 g/8 oz button onions, peeled
225 g/8 oz carrots, sliced
2 tablespoons tomato purée
3 cloves garlic, crushed
300 ml/½ pint red wine
300 ml/½ pint beef stock
bouquet garni
pinch of dried thyme
salt and pepper
450 g/1 lb tomatoes, peeled and chopped
100 g/4 oz black olives, stoned
25 g/1 oz butter
25 g/1 oz plain flour
GARNISH
chopped parsley
triangles of fried bread

Cut the beef into 2.5-cm/1-in cubes. Heat the oil in a flameproof casserole and add the beef, then fry until brown and remove from the pan. Add the bacon, onions and carrots and sauté for 5 minutes. Stir in the tomato purée, garlic, wine, stock, bouquet garni, thyme and seasoning, then bring to the boil.

Return the meat to the casserole, cover and cook in a cool oven (150 c, 300 f, gas 2) for 1½ hours. Add the tomatoes and olives and cook for a further hour. Blend the butter into the flour and gradually whisk into the casserole, a little at a time. Heat through but do not boil. Garnish with chopped parsley and triangles of fried bread before serving. SERVES 4 TO 6

Beef Loaf

— Moya Maynard —

150 ml/¼ pint beef stock
75 g/3 oz fresh brown breadcrumbs
450 g/1 lb lean minced beef
50 g/2 oz onion, finely chopped
¼ teaspoon dried thyme
50 g/2 oz dried milk powder
1 egg, well beaten
2 teaspoons tomato purée
1 tablespoon chopped parsley
1 teaspoon Worcestershire sauce

Mix all the ingredients and shape the mixture into a loaf in the centre of a large piece of foil. Thoroughly seal the edges of the foil over the loaf. Put the parcel in a tin half filled with water and cook in a moderately hot oven (200 c, 400 f, gas 6) for 1 to 1¼ hours. Open the foil and drain off any liquid, then leave to cool in the foil. Serve with salad ingredients. SERVES 6 TO 8

Beef and Bacon Suet Roll

Audrey Ellis

225 g/8 oz self-raising flour
salt and pepper
100 g/4 oz shredded suet
about 175 ml/6 fl oz water
175 g/6 oz skirt steak, chopped
100 g/4 oz rindless bacon, chopped
1 tablespoon chopped parsley

Sift the flour and 1 teaspoon salt into a bowl, stir in the suet and add sufficient water to make a soft dough. Turn out on to a floured surface and knead lightly until smooth. Then roll out to a rectangle about 25 × 30 cm/ 10 × 12 in.

Mix the beef with the bacon and parsley, and sprinkle with pepper. Spread this filling over the pastry, leaving a narrow rim all round the edge. Dampen the edges and roll up like a Swiss roll, pressing the pastry together to seal the filling in.

Wrap the roll in greased foil, allowing room for the pastry to expand and sealing the edges of the foil to make a watertight parcel. Place in a large saucepan and add boiling water to come halfway up the sides of the roll. Cover the pan and boil gently for 2 hours, adding more boiling water to the pan during this time if necessary.

Lift the parcel out of the saucepan and carefully remove the foil. Serve straight away. SERVES 4

Beef and Parsnip Pie

Jane Todd

1 tablespoon oil
1 onion, chopped
2 carrots, chopped
450 g/1 lb minced beef
2 tomatoes, peeled and sliced
salt and pepper
150 ml/¼ pint beef stock
1 kg/2 lb parsnips
50 g/2 oz butter
2 tablespoons milk
TOPPING
2 tablespoons fresh white breadcrumbs
25 g/1 oz cheese, grated

Heat the oil in a pan and sauté the onion in it until softened. Stir in the carrots and beef and cook, stirring, until the beef is lightly browned. Add the tomatoes, seasoning and stock, bring to the boil and simmer gently for 15 minutes.

Meanwhile, peel the parsnips and cook in boiling salted water for 20 to 25 minutes, until tender. Drain, then mash until smooth. Beat in the butter, milk and a generous amount of black pepper.

Spread half the parsnips in the bottom and up the sides of a greased ovenproof dish. Spoon in the beef mixture and spread the remaining parsnips over the top. Sprinkle the surface with a mixture of the breadcrumbs and cheese and cook in a moderately hot oven (190 C, 375 F, gas 5) for 30 to 35 minutes. SERVES 4

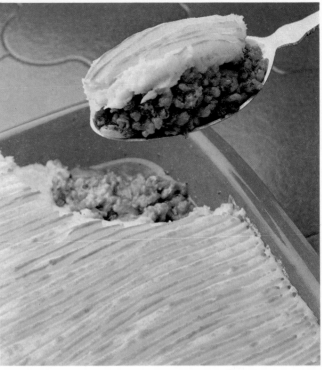

Pasta and Pepper Casserole

— Carol Bowen —

900 g/2 lb stewing steak
50 g/2 oz lard
2 medium onions, chopped
2 teaspoons ground ginger
2 teaspoons soy sauce
1.15 litres/2 pints beef stock
4 tablespoons chopped parsley
salt and pepper
grated rind of 1 large lemon
350 g/12 oz pasta bows or rigatoni
1 (400-g/14-oz) can sweet red peppers,
drained and sliced
chopped parsley to garnish

Cut the stewing steak into bite-sized pieces. Melt the lard in a large frying pan, add the onions and steak and fry until browned on all sides. Transfer to a large flameproof casserole. Add the ginger, soy sauce, beef stock and parsley, then season generously and bring to the boil. Reduce the heat and simmer gently for about 1½ hours or until the meat is tender.

Add the lemon rind, pasta and peppers, then cook gently for a further 15 minutes until the pasta is tender and the excess liquid has been absorbed. Adjust the seasoning, if necessary, before serving sprinkled with chopped parsley. SERVES 6

Shepherd's Pie with Cheesy Potato Topping

— Carol Bowen —

15 g/½ oz butter
2 tablespoons oil
1 medium onion, finely chopped
450 g/1 lb roast beef, minced
150 ml/¼ pint rich beef gravy
2 teaspoons Worcestershire sauce
1 tablespoon chopped parsley
¼ teaspoon dried mixed herbs
salt and pepper
TOPPING
6 tablespoons double cream
40 g/1½ oz butter, melted
2 eggs, lightly beaten
1 kg/2 lb potatoes, boiled and mashed
75 g/3 oz Cheddar cheese, grated

Grease a deep 1.75-litre/3-pint ovenproof dish with the butter. Heat the oil in a saucepan, add the onion and sauté for 5 minutes. Stir in the beef, gravy, Worcestershire sauce, parsley, herbs and seasoning to taste. Transfer to the ovenproof dish.

For the topping, beat the cream, 25 g/1 oz of the butter and the eggs into the hot mashed potato. Add the cheese, mix to blend and season to taste. Pipe or spoon the mashed potato on top of the meat mixture and brush with the remaining melted butter.

Bake in a moderately hot oven (200 C, 400 F, gas 6) for 20 to 25 minutes until golden brown. SERVES 4 TO 6

Veal and Orange Casserole

Julia Roles

1 kg/2 lb stewing veal, trimmed and cubed
salt and pepper
flour for coating
25 g/1 oz butter
1 tablespoon oil
2 onions, sliced
3 carrots, sliced (optional)
2 cloves garlic, crushed
300 ml/½ pint chicken stock
juice of 4 oranges
1 teaspoon lemon juice
1–2 teaspoons arrowroot (optional)
GARNISH
1 tablespoon grated orange rind
chopped parsley

Coat the meat in seasoned flour. Heat the butter and oil in a flameproof casserole and add the veal, onions, carrots, if used, and garlic, then cook gently for 5 minutes. Drain off any excess fat and pour in the stock mixed with the orange and lemon juice. Bring to the boil, cover and cook in a moderate oven (180 C, 350 F, gas 4) for 1½ hours.

The liquid can be thickened with the arrowroot mixed to a paste with a little water. Add the blended arrowroot to the casserole and stir over a gentle heat until the sauce thickens. Garnish with grated orange rind and chopped parsley before serving. SERVES 4 TO 6

Veal with Capers

Moya Maynard

4 veal escalopes
a little seasoned flour
50 g/2 oz butter
juice of ½ lemon
2 tablespoons capers
GARNISH
anchovy fillets, curled
chopped parsley
lemon butterflies

Place the veal between sheets of greaseproof paper and beat it flat. Coat each piece of veal with seasoned flour.

Melt the butter in a frying pan and cook the veal on both sides for about 10 minutes. Remove and keep hot. Add the lemon juice and capers to the pan, heat through and spoon over the veal. Garnish with curled anchovy fillets, chopped parsley and lemon butterflies. SERVES 4

Apricot-stuffed Lamb

— Carol Bowen —

1 (1.75-kg/4-lb) shoulder of lamb, boned
salt and pepper
25 g/1 oz dripping or lard
1 onion, sliced
1 carrot, sliced
bay leaf
300 ml/½ pint chicken stock
STUFFING
50 g/2 oz fresh white breadcrumbs
pinch of dried thyme
25 g/1 oz walnuts, chopped
1 tablespoon oil
1 small onion, chopped
1 (213-g/7½-oz) can apricots
1 egg, beaten

Season the lamb generously and set aside whilst preparing the stuffing.

To make the stuffing, place the breadcrumbs, thyme and walnuts in a bowl. Heat the oil in a small saucepan, then add the onion and cook for about 5 minutes, until soft but not brown. Add to the breadcrumb mixture. Drain and coarsely chop the apricots and stir into the stuffing mixture. Season to taste and bind with sufficient beaten egg to make a moist stuffing. Spoon the stuffing along the shoulder joint and tie it into a long neat shape.

Melt the dripping or lard in a flameproof casserole, add the meat and brown it on all sides. Add the sliced onion, carrot and bay leaf. Pour in the stock and bring to the boil. Cover and cook in a moderate oven (180 c, 350 f, gas 4) for 1½ hours, or until cooked.

Carve the meat and serve with the sieved stock juices poured over the slices. SERVES 6

Lamb Bourguignonne

— Carol Bowen —

1.25 kg/2½ lb boneless lean lamb
350 g/12 oz button onions, peeled
3 tablespoons oil
50 g/2 oz butter or margarine
225 g/8 oz button mushrooms
250 ml/8 fl oz dry red wine
300 ml/½ pint beef stock
½ teaspoon salt
pepper
1 tablespoon arrowroot
1 tablespoon water
GARNISH
chopped parsley
croûtons (see page 17)

Cut the meat into bite-sized pieces. Blanch the onions in boiling water for 2 minutes, then drain.

Heat the oil in a large deep frying pan. Add the butter or margarine and, when foaming, add the meat and brown quickly on all sides. Remove with a slotted spoon and set aside. Add the onions to the pan and brown evenly. Remove with a slotted spoon and mix with the lamb. Finally fry the mushrooms in the pan juices. Return the lamb and onions to the pan. Stir in the wine, stock and seasoning. Bring to the boil, then transfer to a flameproof casserole. Cover and cook in a moderate oven (160 c, 325 f, gas 3) for about 1½ hours or until the meat is cooked. Remove the casserole from the oven.

Dissolve the arrowroot in the water, add slowly to the casserole and cook for a further 5 minutes over a gentle heat, or until the stock is clear and thickened. Adjust the seasoning and serve garnished with chopped parsley and fried bread croûtons. SERVES 6

Curried Minced Lamb

Jane Todd

1 tablespoon oil
2 onions, sliced
2 cloves garlic, crushed
1 tablespoon curry powder
675 g/1½ lb minced lamb
½ teaspoon turmeric
pinch each of ground ginger, paprika and
cayenne pepper
salt and pepper
300 ml/½ pint natural yogurt

Heat the oil in a flameproof casserole and sauté the onions and garlic in it until softened. Stir in the curry powder and cook, stirring, for 2 to 3 minutes. Add the lamb and cook, again stirring, until evenly browned. Add the spices and seasoning and stir in the yogurt, then cover the casserole and simmer for about 1 hour, until cooked.

Serve with rice and a selection of traditional curry side dishes – tomato and onion slices, salted peanuts, chutney and banana slices sprinkled with lemon juice. SERVES 6

Lamb Patties

Jane Todd

6 slices white bread
3 tablespoons milk
3 tablespoons oil
1 onion, chopped
1 clove garlic, crushed
575 g/1¼ lb minced lamb
2 tablespoons chopped parsley
pinch of dried rosemary
salt and pepper
1 egg, lightly beaten
12 rindless rashers streaky bacon
50 g/2 oz butter

Use a 5-cm/2-in cutter to cut out twelve rounds from the slices of bread. Discard the crusts, break up the bread trimmings and place them in a bowl. Pour in the milk and leave to soak. Keep the bread rounds on one side.

Heat 1 tablespoon of the oil in a frying pan and sauté the onion and garlic in it for about 10 minutes, until softened and golden brown. Mix the lamb, parsley, rosemary and cooked onion, season well and bind the ingredients with the beaten egg and soaked bread.

Stretch the bacon rashers with the blade of a knife until they are long and thin. Using floured hands, divide the lamb mixture in twelve equal portions. Shape each portion into a ball, then flatten and shape the meat into cakes measuring 5 cm/2 in. in diameter. Wrap a stretched bacon rasher around each patty and secure with a piece of thread or a wooden cocktail stick. Heat the remaining oil in a large frying pan and fry the patties over a low heat for about 15 minutes on each side. Meanwhile melt the butter in a separate frying pan and fry the bread circles for 2 to 3 minutes on each side, until crisp and brown.

To serve, arrange the bread croûtes on a serving dish. Remove the thread or cocktail sticks from the patties and place each one on a croûte. Serve immediately. SERVES 6

Lamb Pasties

Jane Todd

225 g/8 oz minced lamb
4 spring onions, chopped
1 carrot, grated
pinch of dried rosemary
salt and pepper
SHORTCRUST PASTRY
225 g/8 oz plain flour
¼ teaspoon salt
100 g/4 oz lard *or* 50 g/2 oz lard and 50 g/2 oz
margarine
about 3 tablespoons water
beaten egg to glaze

Mix the lamb, onions, carrot and rosemary with plenty of seasoning.

To make the pastry, sift the flour and salt into a bowl. Rub in the lard or lard and margarine until the mixture resembles fine breadcrumbs, then add the water and mix to make a firm dough. Wrap the dough in cling film and chill for 30 minutes.

Roll out the dough on a lightly floured surface and cut out four 18-cm/7-in circles. Divide the filling between the circles, placing it in the centre of each. Dampen the edges and bring them together at the top to form a pasty. Press the edges together well and crimp them between your fingers. Place the pasties on a greased baking tray and brush with beaten egg. Bake in a hot oven (220 C, 425 F, gas 7) for 15 minutes, then lower the temperature to moderate (190 C, 350 F, gas 4) and bake for a further 15 to 20 minutes, until well browned. Serve hot or cold. SERVES 4

Carré de Porc à l'Orange

Diana Jaggar

2 small (6 bone) best ends of pork, skinned
25 g/1 oz butter · 1 onion, finely chopped
2 sticks celery, finely chopped
100 g/4 oz fresh white breadcrumbs
grated rind of 1 orange
50 g/2 oz seedless raisins
2 teaspoons chopped parsley
salt and pepper
juice of 2 oranges and $\frac{1}{2}$ lemon
50 g/2 oz soft brown sugar
1 tablespoon Worcestershire sauce
150 ml/$\frac{1}{4}$ pint each white wine and chicken stock
2 oranges, sliced and fried in butter to garnish

Ask the butcher to trim the cutlets and make them into a guard of honour. Melt the butter in a saucepan, add the onion and celery and cook until the onion is soft. Remove the pan from the heat and stir in the breadcrumbs, orange rind, raisins, parsley, salt and pepper, and mix well. Bind the ingredients together with the orange juice. Stand the guard of honour in a roasting tin and spoon the stuffing into the middle.

Bring the sugar, any remaining orange juice, lemon juice and Worcestershire sauce to the boil. Spoon over the meat and roast in a moderately hot oven (190 C, 375 F, gas 5) for about 2 hours, basting regularly.

Transfer the cooked pork to a serving dish, place cutlet frills on the bone ends and keep hot. Skim any fat from the juices in the tin, then add the wine and stock. Bring to the boil, season and serve this sauce with the pork. Arrange the halved fried orange slices around the meat. SERVES 6

Grilled Gammon with Marmalade Sauce

Moya Maynard

4 medium gammon steaks, trimmed
a little oil · 1 small onion, chopped
4 tablespoons marmalade
2 teaspoons white wine vinegar
2 teaspoons demerara sugar

Brush the gammon steaks with oil and place them under a moderate grill. Cook gently for 10 to 15 minutes, turning once.

Place the onion in a small saucepan with 1 teaspoon oil, then cook without browning for 5 minutes. Stir in the remaining ingredients, heat gently to dissolve, then boil to reduce. Pour over the gammon and serve. SERVES 4

Pork Ragoût

— Julia Roles —

1 kg/2 lb belly of pork, boned
2 onions, sliced · 225 g/8 oz baby carrots
bay leaf
2 teaspoons chopped fresh sage *or* 1 teaspoon
dried sage
1 tablespoon plain flour
150 ml/¼ pint chicken stock
1 (396-g/14-oz) can peeled tomatoes
salt and pepper
450 g/1 lb fresh peas, shelled
6 medium potatoes, peeled and quartered
1 teaspoon sugar

Cut the meat into strips, removing any excess fat. Fry the strips in a dry heavy-based frying pan over medium heat until brown. Transfer to a large ovenproof casserole.

Sauté the onions in the pork fat until soft, then add to the casserole, together with the carrots and herbs. Sprinkle the flour into the fat remaining in the pan and cook for 1 minute, stirring all the time. Gradually blend in the stock and tomatoes and bring to the boil, stirring. Season then pour over the meat. Cover and place in a moderate oven (160 C, 325 F, gas 3) for 1¼ hours.

Add the peas, potatoes and sugar. Re-cover the casserole and return it to the oven to cook for a further 45 minutes or until the peas and potatoes are tender. Remove the bay leaf before serving. SERVES 6

Pork Fillet au Porto

— Julia Roles —

675 g/1½ lb pork fillet
salt and pepper · 25 g/1 oz plain flour
25 g/1 oz butter · 2 onions, chopped
1 tablespoon Worcestershire sauce
1 tablespoon mushroom ketchup
2 tablespoons redcurrant jelly
2 tablespoons tomato purée
4 tablespoons port
4 tablespoons double cream
chopped parsley to garnish

Remove the outer skin from the pork fillet and cut it into 2.5-cm/1-in slices, then coat the meat with seasoned flour. Melt the butter in a frying pan, add the pork and sauté in the butter until golden. Transfer the meat to an ovenproof casserole. Sauté the onions in the butter remaining in the pan until soft, then transfer them to the casserole with the meat.

Mix all the remaining ingredients, except the cream, and pour over the pork and onions. Cover and cook in a moderate oven (180 C, 350 F, gas 4) for 30 to 40 minutes or until the meat is tender. Serve, topped with the cream and chopped parsley. SERVES 4

Pork Chops Pizzaiola

Carol Bowen

1 teaspoon salt
1 teaspoon freshly ground black pepper
6 pork loin chops, cut 2 cm/$\frac{3}{4}$ in thick
3 tablespoons oil
2 cloves garlic, crushed
1 teaspoon dried basil
1 teaspoon dried thyme
bay leaf
75 ml/3 fl oz dry red wine or dark stock
1 (425-g/15-oz) can peeled tomatoes, drained
and finely chopped
2 tablespoons tomato purée
40 g/1$\frac{1}{2}$ oz butter
3 medium green peppers, deseeded and
finely chopped
1 medium onion, sliced in rings
225 g/8 oz button mushrooms (optional)
4$\frac{1}{2}$ teaspoons cornflour

Rub the salt and pepper into both sides of the pork chops. Set aside.

Heat the oil in a large frying pan with a lid, add the chops and brown for 3 minutes on each side. Remove and set aside.

Add the garlic, basil, thyme and bay leaf to the pan. Pour in the wine or stock and bring to the boil, then stir in the tomatoes and tomato purée. Return the chops to the pan and baste them thoroughly with the sauce. Cover the pan and simmer for 40 minutes, basting the chops from time to time.

Meanwhile, melt the butter in a separate frying pan and add the peppers and onion. Cook, stirring occasionally, for 5 to 10 minutes. Add the mushrooms, if used, and cook for a further 2 to 3 minutes. Add these vegetables to the pork chop mixture and continue to cook, uncovered, for a further 15 minutes.

To serve, remove the pork chops from the pan and place them in a warmed serving dish. Thicken the sauce with the cornflour, blended with a little water, and pour over the pork chops. Serve with boiled noodles. SERVES 6

Roast Pork with Apple and Nut Stuffing

Carol Bowen

25 g/1 oz butter
1 small onion, chopped
50 g/2 oz cashew nuts, coarsely chopped
50 g/2 oz crustless white bread, diced
1 cooking apple, peeled, cored and diced
1 stick celery, chopped
2 teaspoons chopped parsley
salt and pepper
2 teaspoons lemon juice
1 (1.5-kg/3$\frac{1}{2}$-lb) blade or loin of pork, boned
2–3 tablespoons oil
150 ml/$\frac{1}{4}$ pint dry cider

Melt the butter in a small pan and fry the onion and nuts until they are lightly browned, about 5 minutes. Add the bread, apple, celery and parsley. Continue to cook for about 5 minutes or until the apple softens, then season to taste and stir in the lemon juice.

Score the rind of the pork deeply and evenly. Open up the pocket in the bladed joint and spread evenly with the stuffing. Alternatively place the stuffing in the loin. Roll up and secure with string. Place the meat in a greased roasting tin, brush with the oil and sprinkle generously with salt. Roast in a moderately hot oven (200 C, 400 F, gas 6) for 20 to 30 minutes, until the crackling is crisp and golden. Reduce the oven temperature to moderate (180 C, 350 F, gas 4) and cook for a further 1$\frac{1}{2}$ hours.

Transfer the pork to a warmed serving dish and keep hot. Skim any fat from the meat juices in the roasting tin, add the cider and bring to the boil. Simmer for 5 minutes, stirring well to incorporate any meat residue. Season to taste and serve with the pork. SERVES 6

Wholemeal Sausage Pie

Carol Bowen

WHOLEMEAL PASTRY
225 g/8 oz wholemeal flour
pinch of salt
50 g/2 oz butter or margarine
50 g/2 oz lard
3 tablespoons cold water
beaten egg or milk to glaze
FILLING
350 g/12 oz pork sausagemeat
1 small onion, finely chopped
3 tablespoons fresh white breadcrumbs
1 teaspoon dried mixed herbs
2 tomatoes, peeled and chopped
2 hard-boiled eggs, shelled

To make the pasty, mix the flour with the salt in a bowl. Rub the butter or margarine and lard into the flour until the mixture resembles fine breadcrumbs. Add the water and mix to a firm but workable dough. Roll out two thirds of the pastry on a lightly floured surface and use to line a 450-g/1-lb loaf tin.

Prepare the filling by mixing the sausagemeat, onion, breadcrumbs, herbs and tomatoes together. Place half this mixture in the base of the tin. Arrange the two hard-boiled eggs along the centre and cover with the remaining sausagemeat mixture.

Roll out the remaining pastry to form a lid. Dampen the edge of the pastry with water and cover the pie with the pastry lid. Trim and flute the edges. Use any pastry trimmings to make leaves to decorate the top of the pie. Make a small hole in the centre to allow any steam to escape. Brush with beaten egg or milk.

Cook in a moderately hot oven (190 C, 375 F, gas 5) for 1 hour or until cooked. Serve cold with salad. SERVES 6

Baked Pork Chops with Apple and Sage Stuffing

Elizabeth Pomeroy

4 neck or loin pork chops
50 g/2 oz lard or butter
100 ml/4 fl oz dry cider or white wine
STUFFING
2 slices bread
1 medium cooking apple
50 g/2 oz butter or margarine
1 tablespoon finely chopped onion
1 tablespoon finely chopped celery
2 tablespoons chopped salted peanuts
2 teaspoons finely chopped fresh sage *or*
1 teaspoon dried sage
freshly ground pepper
lemon juice to taste
GARNISH
fresh sage sprigs
watercress sprigs

Trim most of the fat off the chops. Cut a large gash from the rind of each chop down to the bone to make a pocket.

For the stuffing, remove the crusts from the bread and cut the slices into dice. Peel, core and dice the apple. Melt the butter or margarine in a small saucepan and add the onion, celery and apple, then fry these until softened. Add the nuts and the bread and continue cooking, stirring, until the apple is softened. Mix in the chopped sage and season with pepper and lemon juice.

Pack the stuffing into the pockets in the chops and secure with small skewers or wooden cocktail sticks. Melt the lard or butter in a shallow flameproof casserole or frying pan and add the chops. Seal them on both sides, then when they are nicely browned, arrange them in an ovenproof gratin dish. Add the cider or wine and bake in a moderate oven (180 C, 350 F, gas 4) for 45 to 50 minutes or until tender. Remove the skewers or cocktail sticks and garnish with sprigs of fresh sage and watercress. Serve with potatoes baked in their jackets. SERVES 4

Note: Neck cutlets of veal can be stuffed and cooked in the same way as the pork chops in this recipe.

Glazed Ham

—— *Audrey Ellis* ——

1 (1.75-g/4-lb) piece middle or corner
gammon
1.15 litres/2 pints water
1 large onion, quartered
bay leaf
6 peppercorns
GLAZE
75 g/3 oz soft brown sugar
2 teaspoons dry mustard
cloves

Soak the gammon overnight in cold water to cover. Next day, drain and discard the water and place the ham in a saucepan with the 1.15 litres/2 pints water, the quartered onion, bay leaf and peppercorns. Cover the pan and bring to the boil, then reduce the heat and simmer for 1½ hours.

Remove the gammon from the cooking liquid and cut off the skin. Mark the fat into diamond shapes with a sharp knife and place in a roasting tin. Mix the sugar and the mustard together and press on to the fat. Stick a clove in the centre of each diamond.

Bake the ham in a hot oven (220 C, 425 F, gas 7) for about 15 minutes or until the fat is crisp and golden. Serve with beans and carrots, if liked. SERVES 8

Bacon and Split Pea Stew

—— *Audrey Ellis* ——

175 g/6 oz dried split peas
small knuckle of green bacon
50 g/2 oz butter
2 onions, chopped
2 carrots, chopped
1.15 litres/2 pints chicken stock
chopped parsley
pepper
3 frankfurter sausages, halved

Soak the peas and the knuckle of bacon separately overnight in cold water to cover. Drain both thoroughly.

Melt the butter in a saucepan, add the chopped onions and carrots and fry gently for 5 minutes. Add the split peas, knuckle of bacon, chicken stock, parsley and pepper to taste. Bring to the boil, then reduce the heat and simmer for 1½ hours.

Remove the knuckle of bacon, take off and chop any meat. Put this back into the stew with the halved frankfurters. Ladle the stew into individual bowls and serve immediately. SERVES 4

Sausage in Mustard Sauce

— *Audrey Ellis* —

4 Cumberland sausages
4 thick rindless rashers lean bacon
2 tablespoons oil
1 onion, sliced
1 tablespoon fine fresh breadcrumbs
600 ml/1 pint Béchamel Sauce (see page 20)
1 tablespoon French mustard
juice of $\frac{1}{2}$ lemon
1 tablespoon sugar
100 g/4 oz button mushrooms, sliced
salt and pepper
GARNISH
1 small tomato, sliced
parsley sprigs

Wrap each sausage in a rasher of bacon and secure with a wooden cocktail stick. Grill for 5 minutes on each side.

Heat the oil in a shallow pan and use to fry the onion gently for 3 minutes. Stir in the breadcrumbs. Add the sauce, French mustard, lemon juice, sugar, mushrooms and seasoning. Bring to the boil, stirring all the time, and add the bacon and sausage rolls.

Cover and simmer for 20 minutes. Remove the cocktail sticks from the sausages and serve immediately, garnished with tomato slices and parsley sprigs. SERVES 4

Sausage and Ale Pie

— *Audrey Ellis* —

50 g/2 oz fat
450 g/1 lb large pork sausages
100 g/4 oz baby onions, peeled
40 g/1$\frac{1}{2}$ oz plain flour
450 ml/$\frac{3}{4}$ pint brown ale
salt and pepper
100 g/4 oz button mushrooms
225 g/8 oz puff pastry
beaten egg to glaze
parsley sprig to garnish

Melt the fat in a frying pan, add the sausages and fry gently for about 8 minutes, until pale golden. Transfer the sausages to a large pie dish. Add the onions to the fat remaining in the pan and fry until golden, then spoon them over the sausages.

Stir the flour into the remaining pan fat and cook it for 3 minutes. Gradually stir in the brown ale and season to taste, then bring to the boil, stirring constantly, add the mushrooms and pour over the sausages.

Roll out the pastry to cover the pie dish. Dampen the rim of the dish and place the pastry lid on top, pressing round the rim to seal. Decorate with pastry trimmings and mark a criss-cross pattern on top with a knife.

Brush with a little beaten egg and bake in a moderately hot oven (200 c, 400 f, gas 6) for about 30 to 40 minutes until golden and well puffed. Serve immediately, garnished with parsley. SERVES 6

Vegetarian Dishes

Vegetarian main dishes are certainly more interesting than a basic nut roast and here are some recipes to prove it. Try, for example, Italian-style Aubergines, Gougère or Coriander Mushrooms for a deliciously different main course.

Vegetable Curry, Gloucester Pie and
Chick Peas with Peppers

Vegetable Curry

Bridget Jones

(ILLUSTRATED ON PREVIOUS PAGE)

1 kg/2 lb fresh and frozen vegetables, for
example 1 small cauliflower, carrots,
potatoes, aubergines, peppers, courgettes and
sweet corn
225 g/8 oz onions
2 tablespoons oil
4 cardamoms
1 cinnamon stick
bay leaf
3 cloves garlic, crushed
2 tablespoons garam masala
½ teaspoon chilli powder
salt and pepper
300 ml/½ pint vegetable stock
2 tablespoons chopped fresh coriander
coriander sprigs to garnish

Prepare your selection of vegetables according to their
type. Finely chop the onions. Heat the oil in a large pan,
add the remaining ingredients, except the stock and
coriander, and cook, stirring continuously, for a few
minutes.

Add the onions to the pan and continue to cook until
they are soft but not browned. Pour in the stock and
bring to the boil, then add the vegetables and cook
gently, covered, until they are tender – about 15 to 20
minutes. Stir in the chopped coriander 5 minutes before
the end of the cooking time, taste and adjust the
seasoning if necessary. Serve garnished with coriander
sprigs. SERVES 4

Chick Peas with Peppers

Bridget Jones

(ILLUSTRATED ON PREVIOUS PAGE)

2 tablespoons oil
1 large onion, chopped
1 red pepper, deseeded and chopped
1 green pepper, deseeded and chopped
1 clove garlic, crushed
salt and pepper
2 (439-g/15½-oz) cans chick peas, drained
2 tablespoons chopped fresh herbs
a little grated nutmeg

Heat the oil in a saucepan. Add the onion, peppers and
garlic, then sprinkle in seasoning to taste and cook until
the vegetables are softened but not browned.

Stir in the chick peas and cook, covered, over a low
heat until they are heated through. Stir in the herbs and
nutmeg to taste before serving. SERVES 4

Walnut Cheese Dolmas

Marguerite Patten

6–8 large, tender cabbage leaves
generous 150 ml/¼ pint water
salt and pepper
STUFFING
50 g/2 oz cooked long-grain rice or fresh
wholemeal breadcrumbs
50 g/2 oz Cheddar cheese, finely grated
50 g/2 oz walnuts, finely chopped
1 tablespoon chopped parsley
1 tablespoon chopped chives
25–50 g/1–2 oz margarine, melted
1 egg
CHEESE SAUCE
25 g/1 oz butter or margarine
25 g/1 oz plain flour
300 ml/½ pint milk
50–100 g/2–4 oz Cheddar cheese, grated

Wash and drain the cabbage leaves. Bring the water to
the boil and add a little salt and pepper. Put in the
cabbage leaves, boil for 1½ to 2 minutes (just long enough
to soften the leaves) and lift from the liquid. Reserve the
cooking liquid. Cool the leaves slightly and spread each
one flat.

Mix the ingredients for the stuffing, adding salt and
pepper to taste. Divide the stuffing between the leaves,
then fold them to enclose the filling. Put the stuffed
cabbage leaves into an ovenproof casserole with the
cabbage stock, cover tightly and cook in the centre of a
moderate oven (160 C, 325 F, gas 3) for 35 to 40 minutes.

Meanwhile make the sauce. Melt the butter or
margarine in a small saucepan, add the flour and cook,
stirring, for a minute. Gradually pour in the milk and
bring to the boil, stirring continuously. Remove the pan
from the heat and stir in the cheese until it melts. Add
seasoning to taste.

Lift the dolmas from the liquid and place them in a
heated serving dish. Top with the cheese sauce and serve
immediately. SERVES 3 TO 4

Italian-style Aubergines

Janet Hunt

2 large aubergines
salt
2 tablespoons oil
1 egg, beaten
100 g/4 oz mozzarella cheese
TOMATO SAUCE
2 tablespoons oil
2 cloves garlic, crushed
450 g/1 lb tomatoes, peeled and chopped *or*
2 (227-g/8-oz) cans tomatoes
1 teaspoon dried oregano
pinch of raw brown sugar
salt and pepper
TOPPING
50 g/2 oz Parmesan cheese, grated

Set the oven at moderately hot (200 c, 400 f, gas 6). Wash, trim and slice the aubergines, lay the slices on a plate and sprinkle them with salt. Leave for 30 minutes, then rinse them thoroughly with fresh water and pat dry.

To make the tomato sauce, heat the oil in a saucepan and add the garlic. Cook for a few minutes, then stir in the remaining ingredients and bring to the boil. Cover and simmer for 15 minutes; blend in a liquidiser or press through a sieve. Set aside.

Heat the oil in a frying pan. Dip the aubergine slices in beaten egg and fry them until lightly coloured on each side. Slice the mozzarella. Arrange the aubergines, tomato sauce and mozzarella in layers in a small greased ovenproof dish until all the ingredients have been used. Sprinkle the Parmesan cheese over the top and bake the aubergines for 20 minutes or until the top begins to brown. Serve with a salad made of endive, chicory and lettuce for a fresh, crisp contrast to a rather rich dish.
SERVES 4

Variations

This dish can also be prepared using other vegetables instead of the aubergines. Try substituting 2 large bulbs fennel (as illustrated) and make the dish in the same way but omitting the salting process. This is only necessary with aubergines as it removes excess water, making the aubergine easier to cook and more able to retain its shape.

Spanish Rice au Gratin

Audrey Ellis

75 g/3 oz brown rice
300 ml/½ pint water
1 teaspoon salt
15 g/½ oz butter
50 g/2 oz onion, chopped
1 small green pepper, deseeded and chopped
50 g/2 oz celery, chopped
1 (227-g/8-oz) can peeled tomatoes
1 teaspoon brown sugar
1 teaspoon chilli powder (or to taste)
100 g/4 oz cheese, grated
GARNISH
about 4 black olives, stoned
parsley sprigs

Place the rice in a saucepan with the water and salt. Bring to the boil, cover and simmer for 30 minutes.

Meanwhile, melt the butter in a saucepan, add the onion, pepper and celery and cook until soft. Stir in the tomatoes and their liquid, the brown sugar and chilli powder. Add the cooked rice and simmer until thick – about 10 minutes.

Transfer the mixture to a greased ovenproof dish and sprinkle the cheese over the top. Place in a moderately hot oven (190 C, 375 F, gas 5) for about 30 minutes to melt and lightly brown the cheese. Serve immediately, garnished with the olives and parsley. SERVES 4

Vegetarian Bean Hotpot

Audrey Ellis

175 g/6 oz red kidney beans
2 large leeks
2 large carrots, sliced
225 g/8 oz potatoes, sliced
1 onion, chopped
salt and pepper
175 g/6 oz cheese, grated
1 clove garlic, crushed
750 ml/1¼ pints vegetable stock
TOPPING
a few slices of French bread
grated cheese
chopped parsley

Soak the kidney beans in cold water to cover overnight, then drain and cook in boiling water for 10 minutes. Drain and set aside. Cut the leeks into rings and rinse well in a colander under running water.

Arrange the beans, leeks, carrots, potatoes and onion in an ovenproof dish. Sprinkle with the seasoning and grated cheese. Stir the crushed garlic into the stock and pour it over the vegetable mixture.

Cover and cook in a cool oven (150 C, 300 F, gas 2) for 2½ hours. Top with the French bread, arranging the slices in an overlapping pattern and sprinkle with the grated cheese. Increase the oven temperature to moderately hot (200 C, 400 F, gas 6) and cook for a further 30 minutes, or until the cheese has melted. Sprinkle with a little chopped parsley and serve. SERVES 4

Lentil-stuffed Courgettes

Janet Hunt

6 medium courgettes
1 onion
2 tomatoes (optional)
2 sticks celery
50 g/2 oz butter or margarine
100 g/4 oz red split lentils
salt and pepper
1–2 teaspoons chopped fresh mixed herbs
or ½–1 teaspoon dried mixed herbs
50 g/2 oz Cheddar cheese, grated

Blanch the courgettes in boiling salted water for 2 to 3 minutes. Drain well, cool slightly and cut the courgettes in half lengthways. Scoop out and chop the flesh.

Chop the onion and the tomatoes, if used, and finely slice the celery. Melt half the butter or margarine in a saucepan and stir in the onion, tomato, celery, and chopped courgette. Sauté all the vegetables together briefly, then add the lentils and enough water to cover.

Bring to the boil, reduce the heat and simmer for about 20 minutes, until the lentils and vegetables are tender and all the water has been absorbed. Season with salt and pepper to taste and sprinkle with herbs. Use the mixture to fill the courgette skins and arrange the stuffed courgettes side by side in a greased ovenproof dish. Sprinkle with cheese and dot with the remaining fat. Grill the courgettes for 5 to 10 minutes, or until golden brown. Serve with young French beans or spinach. SERVES 4

Broccoli and Egg Salad

Janet Hunt

450 g/1 lb broccoli
salt
2 large tomatoes
6 spring onions
about 4 tablespoons mayonnaise
2 hard-boiled eggs, sliced
a little paprika

Break the broccoli into sprigs and cook them in a little boiling salted water until just tender. Drain and rinse the broccoli in cold water, then drain thoroughly and place in a serving bowl.

Quarter the tomatoes, trim and chop the spring onions and add them to the broccoli. Mix in enough mayonnaise to moisten the salad ingredients to taste and top with the sliced eggs. Sprinkle with paprika and serve. SERVES 4

Chestnut Roll

Janet Hunt

PASTRY
100 g/4 oz butter or margarine
225 g/8 oz plain wholemeal flour
pinch of salt
2–3 tablespoons cold water
milk to glaze
FILLING
225 g/8 oz chestnuts
25 g/1 oz butter or margarine
50 g/2 oz mushrooms, chopped
1 leek, finely sliced
½ clove garlic, crushed
1–2 tablespoons water
salt and pepper
watercress to garnish

Rub the butter or margarine into the flour and salt until the mixture resembles fine breadcrumbs. Add enough water to bind the ingredients to a dough, knead lightly and wrap in kitchen foil or cling film. Stand the dough in the refrigerator for at least 30 minutes.

To make the filling, slit the shells of the chestnuts and cook them in boiling water for 15 minutes. Drain and allow to cool, then peel away both the outer shells and the inner skin. Melt the butter or margarine in a pan and sauté the mushrooms briefly; remove and set them aside. Put the sliced leek and garlic together into the pan and sauté gently for 5 minutes. Chop the chestnuts coarsely and add them to the pan. Pour in just enough water to moisten the ingredients, cover the pan and simmer for 10 minutes or until the nuts and leeks are tender. Add more water if necessary, but not too much as the mixture must be dry. Stir in the mushrooms and remove the pan from the heat. Drain thoroughly and season to taste with salt and pepper.

On a lightly floured surface, roll the pastry out to a neat oblong measuring roughly 30 × 23 cm/12 × 9 in and spread the chestnut and vegetables over it, leaving a small space around the edges. Roll up the pastry from the longest edge, like a swiss roll. Dampen the edges with a little water, press them together to seal and place the roll on a lightly greased baking sheet. Brush the top with milk.

Bake the chestnut roll in a moderately hot oven (200 C, 400 F, gas 6) for 30 to 40 minutes, until the pastry is cooked. Serve in thick slices garnished with watercress and accompanied by a creamy white sauce and a cucumber salad, if liked. SERVES 4

Gloucester Pie

Carol Bowen

8 slices bread, crusts removed
75 g/3 oz butter
100 g/4 oz Double Gloucester cheese, thinly
sliced
225 g/8 oz tomatoes, peeled and sliced
150 ml/¼ pint milk
1 egg, beaten
1 teaspoon prepared mustard
salt and pepper
watercress sprigs to garnish

Butter the slices of bread with three-quarters of the butter. Sandwich together, in pairs, with the cheese and tomatoes. Cut each sandwich into four triangles and arrange in a shallow ovenproof dish.

Beat together the milk, egg, mustard and seasoning to taste. Pour over the bread and leave to soak in for 30 minutes. Dot the top with the remaining butter and bake in a moderately hot oven (190 c, 375 f, gas 5) for 25 to 30 minutes or until the top is crisp and golden. Serve garnished with watercress sprigs. SERVES 4

Spiced Egg Ragoût

Carol Bowen

50 g/2 oz butter or margarine
225 g/8 oz button onions, halved
450 g/1 lb potatoes, cut into fingers (or chips)
1 teaspoon chilli seasoning
1 teaspoon ground cardamom
½ teaspoon ground coriander
½ teaspoon turmeric
2 tablespoons plain flour
1 (396-g/14-oz) can peeled tomatoes
1 clove garlic, crushed
300 ml/½ pint vegetable stock
150 ml/¼ pint natural yogurt
salt and pepper
8 hard-boiled eggs, shelled
GARNISH
croûtons (see page 17)
1 tablespoon chopped parsley

Melt the butter in a large saucepan. Add the onions and potatoes and cook until lightly brown. Add the chilli seasoning, cardamom, coriander, turmeric and flour and cook for 1 minute, stirring all the time.

Stir in the tomatoes with their juice, the garlic, stock, yogurt and seasoning to taste. Bring to the boil, then cover the pan and simmer gently for about 40 minutes.

Cut the eggs in half lengthways. Add to the sauce and leave over a low heat to warm through. Mix the croûtons with the chopped parsley and sprinkle over to garnish the dish. Serve with cooked rice or pasta. SERVES 4

Iced Camembert Tart

— Audrey Ellis —

SHORTCRUST PASTRY
225 g/8 oz plain flour
pinch of salt
100 g/4 oz margarine
cold water to mix
FILLING
3 eggs, separated
150 ml/¼ pint single cream
1 ripe Camembert cheese
15 g/½ oz gelatine, dissolved in 2 tablespoons
warm water
GARNISH
parsley sprigs
1 tomato, sliced

To make the pastry, sift the flour into a bowl with the salt. Add the margarine and rub it in until the mixture resembles fine breadcrumbs. Stir in enough water to make a short pastry dough.

Roll out the pastry to line a 20-cm/8-in flan dish, and bake blind for 30 minutes in a moderately hot oven (190 c, 375 f, gas 5). Cool.

Beat together the egg yolks and cream in a small bowl, then stand the bowl over a pan of hot water and cook, stirring constantly, until thickened. Trim away the outer crust from the cheese. Cut the cheese into small dice, add to the egg mixture and stir until dissolved. Remove from the heat and stir in the gelatine. Whisk the egg whites until stiff, fold into the cheese, and pour into the flan.

Chill the flan until the filling is set, then serve cut in wedges, garnished with parsley sprigs and tomato slices. SERVES 4 TO 6

Walnut Cheese Ball

— Audrey Ellis —

225 g/8 oz cream cheese
1½ teaspoons garlic salt or celery salt
1 tablespoon chopped parsley
1 tablespoon grated onion
1 tablespoon chopped green pepper
100 g/4 oz drained canned crushed pineapple
100 g/4 oz walnuts, chopped
TO SERVE
lettuce leaves
cocktail biscuits
olives
tomatoes

Beat the cream cheese until soft and gradually stir in the salt, parsley, onion, green pepper and crushed pineapple. Finally add half the nuts and combine well, then chill in the refrigerator until firm.

Sprinkle the remaining nuts on a sheet of foil. Shape the chilled mixture into a ball and roll in the nuts until evenly coated. Serve the walnut-coated cheese on a bed of lettuce and surround it with cocktail biscuits, olives and tomatoes. SERVES 4

Gougère

Janet Hunt

CHOUX PASTRY
75 g/3 oz plain wholemeal flour
pinch of salt
50 g/2 oz butter or margarine
150 ml/$\frac{1}{4}$ pint water
2 large eggs, lightly beaten
40 g/1$\frac{1}{2}$ oz Cheddar cheese, grated
FILLING
2 tablespoons oil
1 onion, finely chopped
$\frac{1}{2}$ clove garlic, crushed
2 large courgettes
4 large tomatoes
salt and pepper
1–2 tablespoons water
50 g/2 oz cooked peas
chopped fresh parsley or chives to garnish
(optional)

Sift the flour with the salt, reserving the bran from the flour for another recipe. Combine the fat and water in a small saucepan and heat gently until the fat melts. Bring the mixture to the boil and immediately add the flour. Beat the ingredients quickly with a wooden spoon until the mixture forms a dough and comes away from the side of the pan. Leave to cool for a few minutes, then gradually beat in the eggs, a little at a time, and continue beating until the mixture is thick and glossy in texture.

Place the dough in a piping bag fitted with a large plain nozzle and pipe choux buns around the inside edge of a round, greased ovenproof dish. Sprinkle with the grated cheese and bake in a moderately hot oven (200 c, 400 f, gas 6) for 30 to 40 minutes or until well risen.

Heat the oil in a pan and sauté the chopped onion and garlic for 5 to 10 minutes. Slice the courgettes and the tomatoes and add them to the pan with salt and pepper to taste. Sauté the vegetables briefly, then pour in enough water to moisten the pan, cover and simmer the vegetables for 15 to 20 minutes. Stir in the cooked peas and allow them to heat through.

Arrange the gougère on an attractive serving dish and fill the centre with the vegetables. Sprinkle with chopped fresh parsley or chives, if liked, and serve cut into wedges. A cheese or tomato sauce (page 125) goes well with this dish. SERVES 4

Wholemeal Pizza

Carol Bowen

15 g/$\frac{1}{2}$ oz fresh yeast
$\frac{1}{2}$ teaspoon sugar
150 ml/$\frac{1}{4}$ pint lukewarm water
200 g/7 oz wholemeal flour
1 teaspoon salt
2 teaspoons olive oil
TOPPING
1 (396-g/14-oz) can peeled tomatoes, drained
and sliced
salt and pepper
1 tablespoon dried basil
$\frac{1}{2}$ teaspoon garlic salt
175 g/6 oz mozzarella cheese, sliced
8 black olives
1 tablespoon capers

Mix the yeast with the sugar and 2 tablespoons of the water. Leave until frothy.

Combine the flour and salt in a large mixing bowl. Make a well in the centre and pour in the yeast liquid, olive oil and remaining water. Mix in the flour to make a smooth dough. Knead for 5 minutes, then leave to rise, covered, in a warm place until double in size.

Roll out the dough into a 23-cm/9-in circle and place on a greased baking tray. Leave for 10 minutes, then arrange the topping ingredients on the dough and bake in a moderately hot oven (190 C, 375 F, gas 5) for 30 minutes. Serve immediately. SERVES 4 TO 6

Vegetable Lasagne

Carol Bowen

175 g/6 oz lasagne verdi
2 medium onions, sliced
350 g/12 oz tomatoes, peeled and sliced
350 g/12 oz courgettes, halved lengthways and
sliced
3 tablespoons oil
$\frac{1}{2}$ teaspoon dried basil
1 tablespoon tomato purée
salt and pepper
25 g/1 oz walnut pieces, chopped
450 ml/$\frac{3}{4}$ pint natural yogurt
2 eggs
$\frac{1}{4}$ teaspoon ground cumin
75 g/3 oz Cheddar cheese, grated

Cook the lasagne in plenty of boiling salted water for 15 minutes. Drain. Fry the onions, tomatoes and half the courgettes in 1 tablespoon of the oil until the tomatoes soften. Stir in the basil, tomato purée and seasoning. Mix in the walnuts.

Grease a 2-litre/3$\frac{1}{2}$-pint ovenproof dish and layer the vegetable mixture and lasagne in it, ending with a layer of lasagne. Season the yogurt generously and beat in the eggs, cumin and cheese. Pour over the lasagne and top with the remaining courgettes. Brush with the remaining oil and bake in a moderately hot oven (200 C, 400 F, gas 6) for about 40 minutes or until the yogurt is set. Serve immediately. SERVES 4

Parsnip Flan

Janet Hunt

FLAN CASE
1 (198-g/7-oz) packet wholemeal crackers or crispbread
about 75 g/3 oz butter or margarine
50 g/2 oz Cheddar cheese, grated
salt and pepper
FILLING
450 g/1 lb parsnips
2 eggs, beaten
50 g/2 oz Cheddar cheese, grated
pinch of grated nutmeg
2 large tomatoes, sliced

Put the crackers or crispbread into a plastic bag and use a rolling pin to crush them to fine, even-sized crumbs. Melt the butter or margarine in a pan and stir in the crumbs, adding a little more fat if the mixture seems dry. Stir well, add the grated Cheddar and seasoning to taste and remove the pan from the heat. Grease a 20-cm/8-in flan tin and line it with the mixture. Leave in a cool place to firm up.

Peel and chop the parsnips and cook them in boiling salted water for 15 to 20 minutes until tender. Mash them to a purée and leave to cool slightly. Mix in the beaten egg, grated Cheddar, nutmeg and salt and pepper to taste, spoon the mixture into the flan case and arrange the sliced tomatoes on top. Bake in a moderately hot oven (190 C, 375 F, gas 5) for 20 to 30 minutes until the filling is cooked and the flan case crisp. SERVES 4

Scrambled Eggs with Tofu

Janet Hunt

25 g/1 oz butter or margarine
275 g/10 oz tofu, diced
4 eggs
salt and pepper
pinch of paprika
chopped fresh chives to garnish

Melt the butter or margarine in a saucepan. Add the tofu to the pan, mashing it with the fat to make a crumb-like mixture. Sauté for a few minutes.

Beat the eggs with salt and pepper to taste and pour the mixture over the tofu. Cook gently, stirring the eggs up from the bottom of the pan, until the mixture begins to set but is still soft. Remove the pan from the heat and allow the egg to set completely for about 1 minute before serving it on toast or a bed of fresh, lightly steamed spinach. Sprinkle paprika and chopped fresh chives over the top. SERVES 4

Hummus

Carol Bowen

450 g/1 lb cooked or canned chick peas
2 tablespoons olive oil
1 or 2 cloves garlic, crushed
2 teaspoons lemon juice
½ teaspoon paprika
1 tablespoon sesame seeds (optional)
salt

Mash the chick peas well. Add the oil, garlic and lemon juice and beat well, then add the paprika, sesame seeds (if used) and salt to taste. Alternatively, place all the ingredients in a liquidiser and blend to a smooth purée.

Serve with a selection of raw vegetables, such as strips of carrot and celery, cauliflower florets and spring onions. SERVES 4

Coriander Mushrooms

Carol Bowen

225 g/8 oz small button mushrooms
6 tablespoons olive oil
1 teaspoon crushed coriander seeds
2 tablespoons lemon juice
salt and pepper
chopped parsley

Wipe the mushrooms with a damp cloth and cut them into halves or quarters.

Heat 4 tablespoons of the oil in a large frying pan. Add the coriander seeds and fry for about 2 minutes, stirring continuously. Stir in the mushrooms, then cover and cook for 3 to 5 minutes or until tender.

Transfer to a serving dish, and add the remaining oil, lemon juice and seasoning. Chill before serving sprinkled with chopped parsley. SERVES 2

Vegetables and Salad

This chapter is filled with mouth-watering ideas for all seasons: warming vegetable pie for the winter months, crisp and crunchy salads for the spring and summer, and some homely baked potato suggestions for autumnal evenings.

Stuffed Baked Potatoes

(ILLUSTRATED ON PREVIOUS PAGE)

Allow one large potato per person. Thoroughly scrub the potatoes and cut out any eyes or bruised bits. Prick the skin and brush with a little oil. Place the potatoes on a baking tray. Cook in a moderately hot oven (200 c, 400 f, gas 6) for about 1½ hours. The cooking time will depend on the size of the potatoes. When cooked, split the potatoes down the middle and fill with any of the suggested fillings. If you like, cook two small potatoes per person and offer a selection of fillings.

Cream Cheese and Herbs Beat chopped fresh herbs, seasoning and finely chopped spring onions into cream cheese. Shape into a roll, chill thoroughly, then slice thickly. Place two or three slices in each cooked potato.

Cottage Cheese and Ham Mix chopped cooked ham, seasoning and chopped parsley into cottage cheese. Spoon the mixture into the cooked potatoes before serving.

Bacon Rolls Roll up rashers of rindless bacon and secure with wooden cocktail sticks. Grill until golden, then place a couple on each cooked potato and serve immediately.

Seafood Filling Mix peeled cooked prawns with flaked tuna fish and a little mayonnaise. Add lemon juice, seasoning and a little tomato purée to taste. Spoon this mixture into the cooked potatoes.

Provençal Filling Mix roughly chopped peeled tomatoes with finely chopped onion, pitted black olives and plenty of seasoning. Stir in a little olive oil and lemon juice to taste, then spoon into the cooked potatoes.

Salami and Gherkin Filling Arrange two or three cones or rolls of salami in each potato. Add gherkin fans and halved slices of tomato.

Soured Cream and Mock Caviar Spoon a little soured cream into each potato and top with a little lumpfish roe. Add a couple of quartered lemon slices to each one.

Smoked Salmon Place a couple of rolls of smoked salmon in each potato. Top with a couple of small lemon wedges and some parsley. Serve with soured cream or mayonnaise and plenty of black pepper.

Mixed Vegetable Salad

(ILLUSTRATED ON PREVIOUS PAGE)

Arrange a selection of prepared vegetables on a platter. For example, prepare chopped peppers, both green and red, chopped or sliced cucumber, sliced tomatoes, coarsely grated carrots, sliced celery, shredded cabbage, lettuce or endive, lightly cooked cut French beans (cooled), radishes and spring onions. Serve the Herb Dressing separately.

Herb Dressing

(ILLUSTRATED ON PREVIOUS PAGE)

Stir 4 tablespoons chopped mixed fresh herbs into 300 ml/½ pint mayonnaise. Add seasoning, mild mustard and a little sugar to taste. Chill lightly before serving.

Cauliflower au Gratin

— *Bridget Jones* —

(ILLUSTRATED ON PREVIOUS PAGE)

1 medium cauliflower
300 ml/½ pint Béchamel Sauce (page 20)
100 g/4 oz Cheddar cheese, grated
generous pinch of dry mustard
salt and pepper

Trim the cauliflower and break it into florets if you like. Cook the whole cauliflower or the florets in boiling salted water for about 15 minutes. Drain thoroughly.

Prepare the sauce according to the recipe instructions. Stir in most of the cheese, the mustard and seasoning to taste. Place the cauliflower in an ovenproof dish and cover with the sauce. Top with the reserved grated cheese, then bake in a moderately hot oven (200 c, 400 f, gas 6) for about 20 minutes or until the topping is golden. Serve immediately. SERVES 4

Note: This dish is delicious topped with chopped fresh herbs, chopped crisply fried bacon, or chopped cooked ham.

Braised Celery with Walnuts

Diana Jaggar

1 head celery, trimmed and washed
salt and pepper
1 medium onion, finely chopped
50 g/2 oz butter
50 g/2 oz walnut pieces
coarsely grated rind of 1 lemon

Cut the celery diagonally into 4-cm/1½-in sticks, then blanch in boiling salted water for 5 minutes. Sauté the onion in 25 g/1 oz of the butter, then add the celery and sauté gently for 5 to 10 minutes, until tender but still crisp.

Meanwhile, fry the walnuts in the remaining butter for 1 to 2 minutes. Stir in the lemon rind, then add the nut mixture to the celery and toss well. Season to taste. SERVES 4

Cauliflower Amandine

Diana Jaggar

1 medium cauliflower
salt and pepper
75 g/3 oz butter
100 g/4 oz almonds, blanched and shredded
chopped parsley to garnish

Break the cauliflower into florets. Trim, wash and cook them in boiling salted water for 10 to 15 minutes until cooked but still crisp. Drain.

Melt the butter in a frying pan and sauté the almonds until golden brown. Add the cauliflower and season to taste, then toss gently and turn into a serving dish. Sprinkle with parsley before serving. SERVES 4

Vegetable Pie

Marguerite Patten

450 g/1 lb potatoes
450–575 g/1–1¼ lb mixed root vegetables
(not potatoes)
100–175 g/4–6 oz cheese, grated
SAUCE
25 g/1 oz butter
25 g/1 oz plain flour
300 ml/½ pint milk or milk and vegetable
stock
salt and pepper

Cook the potatoes in boiling salted water until tender. When cooked, drain and cream them. Meanwhile, peel the vegetables and cut them into small pieces. Cook in boiling salted water until tender.

To make the sauce, melt the butter in a saucepan and stir in the flour. Gradually pour in the milk, stirring all the time, and bring to the boil. Remove the pan from the heat and stir the mixed vegetables into the sauce. Stir in most of the grated cheese and season to taste.

Pour the vegetable mixture into an ovenproof dish and top with the creamed potato. Sprinkle the remaining cheese over the potato and bake in a moderately hot oven (200 C, 400 F, gas 5) for about 15 minutes, or until golden brown. Serve immediately. SERVES 4

Austrian Cabbage

Elizabeth Pomeroy

1 small cabbage (about 450 g/1 lb)
25–50 g/1–2 oz butter or bacon fat
1 small onion, chopped
1 teaspoon paprika
1 teaspoon caraway seeds
salt and pepper
150 ml/¼ pint soured cream

Discard the coarse outer leaves of the cabbage and cut it into quarters, then remove the stalk from each piece. Shred the cabbage finely, wash and drain it thoroughly, then dry it in a clean towel.

In a flameproof casserole, melt the butter or fat and fry the onion gently until transparent. Add the shredded cabbage and sauté lightly, stirring well. Sprinkle in the paprika, caraway seeds, salt and pepper, then stir in the soured cream.

Cover the casserole and continue cooking very gently on top of the cooker or in a moderate oven (160 C, 325 F, gas 3) for 15 to 20 minutes, until the cabbage is tender. Serve with Hungarian Goulash (page 62), bratwurst, grilled sausages or mackerel. SERVES 4

Cider-baked Onions

Elizabeth Pomeroy

4 medium onions
40 g/1½ oz butter *or* 2 tablespoons olive oil
2 teaspoons chopped fresh lemon thyme *or*
1 teaspoon dried lemon thyme
2 teaspoons chopped fresh sage *or*
1 teaspoon dried sage
salt and pepper
3–4 tablespoons cider
chopped fresh thyme or other fresh herbs to
garnish

Peel the onions, cut off the roots and slice off the top. Cut the onions across in half. Melt the butter or heat the oil in a shallow flameproof casserole or gratin dish. Place the onions, centre downwards, in the casserole and fry until golden. Remove from the heat, turn the onions upwards, sprinkle with the herbs and season well with salt and pepper. Pour in sufficient cider to cover the base of the casserole, then cover with a lid or foil.

Bake in a moderately hot oven (190 C, 375 F, gas 5) for 45 minutes to 1 hour, according to size, until tender. Just before serving, spoon the cooking liquid over the onions and sprinkle with fresh herbs. SERVES 4

Minted Tomato Ratatouille

Carol Bowen

450 g/1 lb tomatoes
225 g/8 oz courgettes
225 g/8 oz onions
100 g/4 oz button mushrooms
1 green pepper, deseeded
4 tablespoons oil
2 tablespoons chopped fresh mint
salt and pepper
grated Parmesan cheese

Peel and quarter the tomatoes, and remove the seeds, reserving the juices. Wipe the courgettes and cut them into 5-mm/¼-in slices. Slice the onions and mushrooms. Slice the pepper thinly.

Heat the oil in a large saucepan and fry the courgettes and onions, stirring, until golden. Add half the tomatoes and their juices, the mushrooms, green pepper, mint and salt and pepper to taste. Cover and simmer gently for 15 minutes.

Stir in the remaining tomatoes and reheat gently for about 5 minutes. Serve hot or cold, with Parmesan cheese. SERVES 4

Minty New Potatoes with Cucumber

Diana Jaggar

450 g/1 lb small new potatoes, washed and
scraped
few mint sprigs
salt and pepper
½ large cucumber, peeled
50 g/2 oz butter
2 teaspoons chopped fresh mint
150 ml/¼ pint single cream (optional)

Cook the potatoes, with the mint sprigs, in boiling salted
water for 10 to 15 minutes or until just tender. Quarter
the cucumber lengthwise and cut across into cubes. Melt
the butter in a pan and sauté the cucumber for 5 minutes.
Add the drained cooked potatoes and chopped mint.
Season to taste and toss thoroughly. Add the cream, if
used, and heat to just below boiling. Turn into a serving
dish and serve immediately. SERVES 4 TO 6

Fantail Potatoes

Diana Jaggar

6 medium potatoes, peeled and shaped into
even-sized ovals
1 slice lemon
50 g/2 oz butter
1 onion, finely chopped
salt and pepper
25 g/1 oz Parmesan cheese, grated
25 g/1 oz Cheddar cheese, grated
parsley sprigs to garnish

Slice the potatoes thinly into vertical slices, leaving them
attached at the base. Soak the potatoes in cold water with
a slice of lemon added, until they are all sliced. Melt the
butter in a frying pan and fry the onion until soft.

Drain the potatoes and arrange them, cut side upwards,
in an ovenproof dish. Spoon the onion and butter over
and season to taste. Cook at the top of a moderately hot
oven (190 C, 375 F, gas 5) for 30 minutes, basting
occasionally.

Mix the cheeses and sprinkle over the potatoes. Cook
for a further 20 to 30 minutes until crisp and golden.
Serve immediately. SERVES 6

Tuna Bean Salad

Rosemary Wadey

2 green eating apples, cored and chopped
1 tablespoon lemon juice
1 (198-g/7-oz) can tuna, drained and flaked
1 tablespoon finely chopped onion
3 sticks celery, sliced
1 (425-g/15-oz) can red kidney beans, drained
salt and pepper
4–5 tablespoons French dressing
watercress to garnish

Dip the apple in the lemon juice, then place in a bowl with the tuna, onion, celery and red kidney beans. Season well, add the dressing and toss thoroughly. Leave to stand for about 30 minutes before serving on individual plates. Garnish with watercress and serve with French bread and butter. SERVES 4 TO 6

Salad Niçoise

Rosemary Wadey

a few lettuce leaves
1 (198-g/7-oz) can tuna, drained and flaked
1 green pepper, deseeded and sliced
1 tablespoon finely chopped onion
3 large tomatoes, each cut into six wedges
175 g/6 oz French beans, cooked
1 tablespoon capers
6 tablespoons French dressing
GARNISH
3 hard-boiled eggs
$\frac{1}{2}$ (50-g/1$\frac{3}{4}$-oz) can anchovy fillets, drained
a few black olives

Arrange the lettuce leaves on six small plates or dishes. Lightly toss together the tuna, green pepper, onion, tomatoes, beans, capers and dressing. Spoon the salad over the lettuce leaves. Cut the eggs into quarters and arrange them on the salads with the anchovy fillets and black olives. Serve with French bread. SERVES 6

Ham and Egg Salad

Marguerite Patten

2 or 3 hard-boiled eggs
1 lettuce
100–175 g/4–6 oz cooked ham or boiled bacon
1 (312-g/11-oz) can mandarin oranges
2 tablespoons mayonnaise
a little chopped parsley
1 bunch radishes, trimmed
1 red or green pepper

Shell the hard-boiled eggs and cut them into neat slices.

Arrange the lettuce on a flat dish. Cut the ham or bacon into neat cubes and mix with with the well-drained mandarin oranges and a little of the mayonnaise. Pile the ham mixture into the centre of the lettuce; top with a spoonful of mayonnaise and parsley.

Wash, dry, then slice the radishes and arrange them on top of the sliced eggs around the salad. Cut the stalk end off the pepper, remove the seeds and core, then cut the flesh into neat rings. Arrange on the lettuce. SERVES 4

Nutty Cheese Salad

Jane Todd

4 dessert apples
juice of 1 lemon
50 g/2 oz walnuts, chopped
50 g/2 oz sultanas
2 sticks celery, chopped
100 g/4 oz white cabbage, finely shredded
100 g/4 oz Cheddar cheese, grated, or blue cheese, crumbled
salt and pepper
150 ml/$\frac{1}{4}$ pint natural yogurt or soured cream
chopped parsley to garnish (optional)

Quarter, core and slice the apples, place in a bowl and sprinkle with the lemon juice. Mix in the walnuts, sultanas, celery, cabbage and cheese. Season to taste.

Add the yogurt or soured cream and stir gently until the mixture is evenly coated. Spoon into a serving dish and garnish with lots of chopped parsley, if used. Chill lightly before serving. SERVES 4 TO 6

Cheese and Ham Cornets

Jane Todd

100 g/4 oz cream cheese
25 g/1 oz walnuts, chopped
2 tablespoons chopped parsley or chives
1 tablespoon mayonnaise
salt and pepper
4 slices cooked ham
watercress to garnish

Beat the cream cheese to soften it. Mix in the chopped walnuts, parsley or chives and mayonnaise. Season to taste.

Form each slice of ham into a cornet shape and secure with a wooden cocktail stick. Divide the cream cheese mixture between the ham cornets and chill lightly.

Place the chilled ham cornets on a serving platter and garnish with watercress. SERVES 4

Garlic Sausage and Cheese Salad

Jane Todd

175 g/6 oz Gruyère cheese
175 g/6 oz garlic sausage
$\frac{1}{4}$ cucumber
4 tablespoons mayonnaise
pinch of dry mustard
pinch of paprika
salt and pepper
50 g/2 oz cooked pasta
few lettuce leaves (optional)
chopped parsley or chives to garnish

Cut the cheese, garlic sausage and cucumber into cubes. Mix the mayonnaise with the mustard, paprika and seasoning. Toss the cubed ingredients and pasta in the mayonnaise mixture.

Line a salad bowl with the lettuce leaves, if used, and spoon in the salad. Garnish with lots of parsley or chives and chill lightly before serving. SERVES 4

Cracked Wheat Salad

— Carol Bowen —

100 g/4 oz cracked wheat
2 tablespoons finely chopped shallots or
spring onions
6 tablespoons chopped parsley
6 tablespoons chopped mint
2 tablespoons olive oil
2 tablespoons lemon juice
salt and pepper
black olives
2 tomatoes, sliced

Place the cracked wheat in a bowl and cover with cold water. Leave to soak for 30 minutes. Drain, then wrap in a tea towel and squeeze to extract as much moisture as possible.

Mix the wheat with the shallots or spring onions, parsley, mint, oil and lemon juice. Season to taste with salt and pepper. Place the mixture in a shallow serving dish and garnish with black olives and sliced tomatoes. SERVES 4

Simple Bean Sprout Salad

Crunchy, fresh bean sprouts can be used to make a delicious salad. Mixed with a variety of ingredients – chopped gherkins, chopped canned red pepper, chopped spring onions or green peppers, or even chopped mixed nuts – the sprouts can be dressed with a light mixture of oil and vinegar, seasoned yogurt or mayonnaise.

Lentil and Mung Bean Salad

— Janet Hunt —

1 small onion
1 small green pepper, deseeded
$\frac{1}{4}$ cucumber
100 g/4 oz cooked brown lentils
100 g/4 oz cooked mung beans
LEMON AND HONEY DRESSING
2 tablespoons oil
2 tablespoons clear honey
2 tablespoons lemon juice
salt and pepper
about 4 tablespoons natural yogurt to serve

Chop the onion, green pepper and cucumber and mix them in a bowl with the lentils and mung beans. Mix the oil, honey, lemon juice and seasoning to make the dressing, then pour this over the salad. Leave to marinate for 1 to 2 hours.

Stir in enough yogurt to give the beans a creamy coating and serve the salad on a bed of shredded cabbage, if liked. SERVES 4

Hot Cabbage Salad

— Janet Hunt —

$\frac{1}{2}$ white cabbage
3 carrots
1 onion
2 tablespoons vegetable oil
2 tablespoons seedless raisins
1 teaspoon marjoram *or* $\frac{1}{2}$ teaspoon dried
marjoram
pinch of raw brown sugar
salt and pepper
150 ml/$\frac{1}{4}$ pint natural yogurt
50 g/2 oz chopped nuts (optional)

Shred the cabbage. Slice the carrots and onion as finely as possible. Heat the oil in a large frying pan and gently fry the vegetables and raisins for 3 to 4 minutes, stirring continuously.

Mix the herbs, sugar and seasoning to taste into the yogurt and stir the mixture into the vegetables with the chopped nuts, if used. Heat through very gently for a minute, then serve at once. SERVES 4

Crunchy Bacon Salad

—— Moya Maynard ——

4 slices white bread, cut 1 cm/$\frac{1}{2}$ in thick
50 g/2 oz butter or margarine
5 tablespoons oil
8 rindless rashers streaky bacon
225 g/8 oz button mushrooms, thickly sliced
$\frac{1}{2}$ small onion
salt and pepper
pinch of dry mustard
tablespoon vinegar
50 g/2 oz pimento-stuffed olives, sliced
2 tablespoons chopped parsley

Remove the crusts from the bread and cut the slices into large cubes. Melt the butter or margarine in a frying pan with 2 tablespoons of the oil. Heat gently and fry the bread cubes, turning frequently, until crisp and golden. Remove and drain on absorbent kitchen paper.

Cut the bacon into large pieces, then fry them in any fat remaining in the pan until slightly crisp. Remove from the pan and drain well. Add the mushrooms to the pan and cook slowly until just soft. Remove from the pan, drain and place in a salad bowl.

Grate the onion and add to the mushrooms with the seasoning and mustard. Blend the remaining oil and vinegar into the mushroom mixture. Leave to cool, then stir in the olives, parsley, bacon and cubes of bread. Serve immediately. SERVES 4

Malayan Curried Salad

—— Moya Maynard ——

100 g/4 oz long-grain rice
150 ml/$\frac{1}{4}$ pint mayonnaise
1–2 teaspoons concentrated curry sauce
1 (226-g/8-oz) can pineapple slices, drained
1 small green pepper, deseeded and diced
225 g/8 oz cooked chicken, diced
25 g/1 oz seedless raisins
chopped green pepper to garnish

Cook the rice in boiling salted water for 12 to 15 minutes until tender. Drain well and spread on absorbent kitchen paper to cool.

Mix the mayonnaise with the curry sauce. Cut the pineapple into small pieces and add to the mayonnaise with the green pepper, chicken and raisins. Stir to coat evenly.

Place the rice on a serving dish and top with the curried chicken mixture. Garnish with chopped green pepper. SERVES 3 TO 4

Artichokes Niçoise

Rosemary Wadey

1 (425-g/15-oz) can artichoke hearts, drained
2 tablespoons chopped onion
150 ml/¼ pint French dressing
salt and pepper
1 (50-g/1¾-oz) can anchovy fillets, drained
12 black olives
watercress to garnish

Cut the artichoke hearts into halves or quarters, depending on size, and place in a bowl with the onion, dressing and seasoning. Cut the anchovies into 2.5-cm/ 1-in lengths and add them to the artichokes together with the olives. Toss lightly and leave the salad to stand for about 20 minutes. Arrange in four small dishes and garnish with watercress. SERVES 4

Chinese Salad

Diana Jaggar

½ cucumber, peeled
225 g/8 oz bean sprouts, washed and drained
2 red peppers, halved, deseeded and finely sliced
1 (198-g/7-oz) can sweet corn, drained
2 teaspoons chopped parsley
LEMON DRESSING
2 tablespoons lemon juice
4 tablespoons olive oil
2 tablespoons soy sauce
2 tablespoons single cream
salt and pepper
sugar to taste
chopped parsley to garnish

Cut the cucumber into matchstick strips. Mix these with the bean sprouts, peppers, sweet corn and parsley.
Put all the dressing ingredients into a screw-topped jar and shake well, adding seasoning and sugar to taste. Pour the dressing over the salad and toss well. Serve piled into individual bowls with a little extra parsley sprinkled on top. SERVES 4 TO 6

Chinese Leaves and Avocado Salad

Janet Hunt

1 small head Chinese leaves
1 small green pepper, deseeded
2 sticks celery
½ small red cabbage
2 tomatoes
1 large avocado
50 g/2 oz seedless raisins
TOFU DRESSING
175 g/6 oz tofu
2 tablespoons oil
2 tablespoons cider vinegar
soy sauce *or* salt and pepper
50 g/2 oz flaked almonds, toasted, to garnish

Chop the Chinese leaves, pepper, celery and red cabbage. Quarter the tomatoes. Peel and halve the avocado, remove the stone and slice the flesh. Mix all the prepared ingredients together in a bowl and add the raisins. Mix all the dressing ingredients and pour over the salad. Stir well, then sprinkle with the flaked almonds before serving. SERVES 4

Three Bean Salad

Janet Hunt

100 g/4 oz French beans
1 large onion
100 g/4 oz cooked kidney beans
100 g/4 oz cooked chick peas
1 small clove garlic, finely chopped
6 tablespoons French dressing
¼ leek *or* 1 small green pepper
salt and pepper

Top and tail the French beans and cut them into 2.5-cm/1-in pieces. Cook them in a little boiling salted water for 10 to 15 minutes, until just tender. Drain and leave to cool. Slice the onion. Mix the French beans, kidney beans, chick peas, onion and the garlic together in a bowl, pour in the French dressing and toss well. Leave the salad in a cool place for at least a few hours, preferably 1 to 2 days, so that the beans can absorb all the flavours. Just before serving, finely shred the leek or green pepper, removing the seeds from the pepper. Season the salad and sprinkle the shredded leek or pepper over the top. SERVES 4

Orange and Apple Salad

Marguerite Patten

1 orange
1 tangerine
a few lettuce leaves
1 dessert apple
French dressing
a few nuts

Peel the orange, removing the pith. Divide into neat segments, discarding the pips. Peel and segment the tangerine. Arrange the fruit on the lettuce leaves like the petals of a flower. Quarter, core and dice the apple. Coat the apple in French dressing to taste, add the nuts and spoon the prepared mixture into the centre of the salad. SERVES 2 TO 3

Russian Salad

Marguerite Patten

about 450 g/1 lb mixed root vegetables
1 tablespoon oil
1 tablespoon vinegar
3–4 tablespoons mayonnaise
salt and pepper

Prepare the vegetables and cut them into neat dice. Put into boiling salted water and cook steadily until tender, then strain and allow to cool. Put the cooked vegetables into a basin and mix in the oil and vinegar, then add the mayonnaise. Season to taste and serve. SERVES 4

Rice and Pasta

Rice and pasta can be quickly transformed into exciting dishes with an international flavour, from spicy Lamb Pilaff and Special Chow Mein to more familiar spaghetti dishes, and the recipes are all here to try.

Special Chow Mein, Pullao with Almonds and Pasta alla Carbonara

Pullao with Almonds

Bridget Jones

(ILLUSTRATED ON PREVIOUS PAGE)

50 g/2 oz butter
25 g/1 oz flaked almonds
1 onion, chopped
1 cinnamon stick
4 cardamoms
2 bay leaves
225 g/8 oz long-grain rice
100 g/4 oz dried apricots
600 ml/1 pint water
50 g/2 oz frozen peas

Melt the butter in a saucepan. Add the almonds and cook gently until they are golden, then remove from the pan with a slotted spoon and set aside. Add the onion and spices to the butter remaining in the pan and cook, stirring frequently, until soft but not browned.

Add the bay leaves and rice and stir in the apricots. Pour in the water and bring to the boil. Cover the pan and cook gently for 15 to 20 minutes or until the rice is tender and all the water has been absorbed. About 5 minutes before the end of the cooking time stir in the peas. Add the almonds when the rice has cooked and fluff up the grains with a fork. Serve immediately. SERVES 4

Pasta alla Carbonara

Bridget Jones

(ILLUSTRATED ON PREVIOUS PAGE)

450 g/1 lb pasta (spaghetti, noodles or shapes)
salt and pepper
50 g/2 oz butter
350 g/12 oz cooked ham, cut into strips
100 g/4 oz mushrooms, sliced
1 egg
300 ml/$\frac{1}{2}$ pint single cream
a little chopped parsley to garnish

Cook the chosen pasta in plenty of boiling salted water until just tender – about 10 to 15 minutes.

Meanwhile, melt the butter in a large frying pan and add the ham. Cook until it is a dark pink, then add the mushrooms and toss well in the butter. Cook gently for a few minutes.

Beat the egg thoroughly and stir in the cream. Add seasoning to taste to the ham mixture. Strain the pasta and place it on a heated serving dish or individual plates. Pour the cream mixture over the ham and cook gently, stirring continuously, until heated through. Do not allow the mixture to overheat or it will curdle. Pour the mixture over the pasta and serve immediately, sprinkled with a little parsley if you like. SERVES 4 TO 6

Special Chow Mein

Bridget Jones

(ILLUSTRATED ON PREVIOUS PAGE)

350 g/12 oz Chinese egg noodles
2 tablespoons oil
100 g/4 oz boneless pork, diced
100 g/4 oz boneless chicken meat, diced
100 g/4 oz peeled prawns
50 g/2 oz canned water chestnuts, sliced
1 bunch spring onions, chopped
a little light soy sauce

Cook the noodles in plenty of boiling salted water for about 5 to 10 minutes or until they are just tender. Drain and set aside.

Heat the oil in a large frying pan or wok and add the pork and chicken. Stir-fry until the meats are lightly browned, then add the prawns and water chestnuts, and cook for a few minutes. Stir in the cooked noodles and toss them with the ingredients until they are heated through. Add the spring onions and soy sauce to taste, then serve immediately. SERVES 4

Lamb Pilaff

Jane Todd

50 g/2 oz butter
3 onions, sliced
675 g/1$\frac{1}{2}$ lb minced lamb
50 g/2 oz pine nuts
50 g/2 oz seedless raisins
225 g/8 oz long-grain rice
2 tomatoes, peeled and sliced
900 ml/1$\frac{1}{2}$ pints chicken stock or water
2 tablespoons chopped parsley
$\frac{1}{2}$ teaspoon dried sage
$\frac{1}{4}$ teaspoon ground coriander
$\frac{1}{4}$ teaspoon ground cinnamon
salt and pepper
chopped parsley to garnish

Melt the butter in a flameproof casserole and sauté the onions until softened. Add the lamb and continue cooking until browned. Stir in the pine nuts, raisins, rice and tomatoes. Pour in the stock or water, herbs, spices and seasoning, then bring to the boil and lower the heat. Cover and simmer gently for about 25 minutes, until the rice is tender and the liquid absorbed.

Remove the lid and fork the mixture over the heat to dry off any excess moisture. Turn into a serving dish and garnish with chopped parsley. Serve with a selection of salads. SERVES 6

Seafood Paella

Carol Bowen

2 chicken portions, skinned
3 tablespoons oil
225 g/8 oz lean pork, cubed
225 g/8 oz piece garlic sausage, cubed
1 medium onion, chopped
3 tomatoes, peeled and chopped
450 g/1 lb long-grain rice
225 g/8 oz peas
1 red pepper, deseeded and chopped
salt and pepper
pinch of powdered saffron or turmeric
900 ml/1½ pints chicken stock
2 tablespoons chopped parsley
225 g/8 oz peeled prawns
12–15 cooked mussels
a few unpeeled prawns to garnish

Cut the chicken flesh into bite-sized pieces. Heat the oil in a deep frying pan or paella pan and add the chicken, pork and sausage. Sauté for 5 minutes over a high heat. Add the onion and continue to cook gently over a low heat for 5 minutes, stirring from time to time. Stir in the tomatoes and cook for 3 minutes, then add the rice. Cook, stirring continuously, for a further 5 minutes.

Stir in the peas, red pepper, seasoning and saffron or turmeric, then add the stock. Bring to the boil, cover and simmer for about 20 minutes until all the liquid has been absorbed and the rice is tender. Stir from time to time during the cooking.

Place in an ovenproof dish and stir in the parsley,

prawns and mussels. Cover and cook in a moderate oven (160 C, 325 F, gas 3) for 5 to 10 minutes. Serve garnished with unpeeled prawns. SERVES 4 TO 6

Chicken Pilaff

Carol Bowen

50 g/2 oz butter
25 g/1 oz plain flour
1 (426-ml/15-fl oz) can evaporated milk *or*
400 ml/14 fl oz milk
300 ml/½ pint chicken stock
salt and pepper
450 g/1 lb cooked chicken meat, cut into bite-sized pieces
450 g/1 lb cooked long-grain rice
(about 225 g/8 oz uncooked weight)
100 g/4 oz button mushrooms, sliced
1 green pepper, deseeded and chopped
1 red pepper, deseeded and chopped
1 tablespoon chopped parsley

Melt the butter in a medium-sized saucepan. Add the flour and cook for 1 minute, then gradually stir in the evaporated milk or ordinary milk and the stock to make a smooth sauce. Bring to the boil and simmer for 2 minutes, stirring. Season to taste.

Stir in the chicken, rice, mushrooms, peppers and parsley. Turn into a 1.75-litre/3-pint ovenproof casserole, cover and cook in a moderate oven (180 C, 350 F, gas 4) for 45 minutes. Taste and adjust the seasoning, then serve straightaway. SERVES 6

Danish Pilaff

— Moya Maynard —

25 g/1 oz butter or margarine
1 tablespoon oil
1 medium onion, chopped
2 sticks celery, sliced
175–225 g/6–8 oz forehock bacon steak
225 g/8 oz long-grain rice
450–600 ml/$\frac{3}{4}$–1 pint chicken stock
50 g/2 oz sultanas
1 medium green pepper
toasted flaked almonds to garnish

Place the butter and oil in a frying pan, add the onion and celery and cook slowly until soft – about 10 minutes.

Remove the rind from the bacon and cut the meat into small strips. Add to the pan and cook slowly, stirring, for about 5 minutes. Stir in the rice and cook for 2 minutes until the rice is opaque. Add 450 ml/$\frac{3}{4}$ pint of the chicken stock and cook gently, stirring occasionally, for 20 minutes; add the extra stock if the rice becomes too dry.

Stir in the sultanas. Cut the pepper into strips, removing seeds and pith, and add to the rice. Cook for a further 10 minutes. Spoon the pilaff on to a serving dish and sprinkle with the toasted almonds. SERVES 4

Vegetable Risotto

— Moya Maynard —

2 tablespoons corn oil
100 g/4 oz onions, sliced
2 carrots, diced
15 g/$\frac{1}{2}$ oz dried peppers
1 tablespoon yeast extract
1 litre/1$\frac{3}{4}$ pints boiling water
175 g/6 oz long-grain rice
2 tablespoons tomato purée
25 g/1 oz sultanas
100 g/4 oz peas
grated cheese to serve

Heat the oil in a frying pan, add the onions and sauté gently for about 5 minutes. Add the carrots and cook for a further 5 minutes. Stir in the dried peppers, vegetable extract and boiling water. Add the rice, tomato purée and sultanas, then cook for about 20 minutes, stirring occasionally. Check the risotto during cooking and add a little extra water if necessary. Stir in the peas and cook for about 10 minutes.

Serve immediately, sprinkled with grated cheese. SERVES 4

Risotto with Leeks and Bacon

Carol Bowen

450 g/1 lb rindless streaky bacon, chopped
4 tablespoons oil
4 leeks, chopped
450 g/1 lb long-grain rice
1 (396-g/14-oz) can peeled tomatoes
salt and pepper
$\frac{1}{2}$ teaspoon cayenne pepper
$\frac{1}{2}$ teaspoon ground cumin
1 teaspoon grated lemon rind
900 ml/1$\frac{1}{2}$ pints chicken stock
15 g/$\frac{1}{2}$ oz butter
grated Parmesan cheese (optional)

Dry-fry the bacon in a large saucepan for 8 minutes, or until crisp and golden. Remove from the pan with a slotted spoon and set aside. Add the oil to the bacon fat in the saucepan and fry the leeks for about 12 minutes. Stir in the rice and fry for a further 5 minutes, stirring frequently. Add the tomatoes with their can juice, seasoning to taste, the cayenne, cumin, lemon rind and stock, and bring to the boil.

Return the chopped bacon to the pan, cover and simmer for 15 to 20 minutes, or until the rice is cooked and has absorbed all the liquid. Serve at once, dotted with the butter and sprinkled with the Parmesan cheese, if used. SERVES 4

Rice and Chicken Cakes

Audrey Ellis

225 g/8 oz cooked long-grain rice
150 ml/$\frac{1}{4}$ pint Béchamel Sauce (page 20)
50 g/2 oz nuts (for example almonds, walnuts or peanuts), chopped
175 g/6 oz cooked chicken, chopped
50 g/2 oz sultanas
1 teaspoon curry powder
2 egg yolks
salt and pepper
a little plain flour
1 egg, beaten
toasted breadcrumbs for coating
oil for deep frying
GARNISH
lettuce heart
watercress sprigs
quartered lemon slices

Mix the cooked rice, sauce, nuts, chopped chicken, sultanas, curry powder and egg yolks. Season well with salt and a little pepper. Form into 8 square cakes and chill for 2 to 3 hours.

Coat the cakes in flour, dip into beaten egg and coat with breadcrumbs, taking care that the cakes are completely sealed. Heat the oil for deep frying to 190 c/ 375 F, add the cakes, one or two at a time, and cook until crisp and golden. Drain on absorbent kitchen paper.

Garnish the cakes with a few leaves from the heart of a lettuce, watercress sprigs and quartered lemon slices. Serve immediately. SERVES 4

Rice Moussaka

Audrey Ellis

175 g/6 oz long-grain rice
salt and pepper
2 tablespoons oil
1 onion, chopped
225 g/8 oz minced beef
1 tablespoon tomato purée
4 tomatoes, chopped
150 ml/¼ pint beef stock
600 ml/1 pint Béchamel Sauce (page 20)
100 g/4 oz cheese, grated
GARNISH
1 tomato, sliced
parsley sprig

Cook the rice in plenty of boiling salted water for 15 to 20 minutes, until just tender. Drain and set aside.

Meanwhile, heat the oil, add the onion and fry gently for a few minutes. Add the minced beef and cook, stirring, until browned. Stir in the tomato purée, chopped tomatoes and stock. Season to taste and simmer for 15 minutes.

Mix the Béchamel sauce with the cooked rice and half the grated cheese. Spoon half the mixture into an ovenproof dish and cover with the meat. Top with the remaining rice mixture and sprinkle with the rest of the cheese. Bake in a moderately hot oven (190 C, 375 F, gas 5) for 30 minutes, until lightly browned on top. Serve immediately, garnished with tomato slices and a sprig of parsley. SERVES 6

Cannelloni with Chicken Livers

Audrey Ellis

225 g/8 oz cannelloni
salt and pepper
3 tablespoons oil
225 g/8 oz chicken livers, chopped
1 onion, finely chopped
50 g/2 oz mushrooms, chopped
1 egg, beaten
2 tablespoons savoury stuffing mix
3 tablespoons single cream
300 ml/½ pint Béchamel Sauce (page 20)
50 g/2 oz cheese, grated
GARNISH
tomato slices
watercress sprigs

Cook the cannelloni in plenty of boiling salted water for 8 minutes, until just tender. Drain thoroughly.

Meanwhile, heat the oil in a frying pan. Add the chicken livers and onion and fry for 10 minutes. Stir in the mushrooms and cook for 5 minutes. Off the heat, stir in the beaten egg, stuffing mix and seasoning to taste.

Split each tube of cannelloni lengthways, fill with the meat mixture and roll up. Arrange in a greased ovenproof dish. Stir the cream into the sauce, spoon over the cannelloni and sprinkle with the cheese. Bake in a moderate oven (180 C, 350 F, gas 4) for 30 minutes. Serve immediately, garnished with tomato slices and watercress sprigs. SERVES 4

Chicken Rice Ring

—— Carol Bowen ——

225 g/8 oz long-grain rice
salt and pepper
25 g/1 oz butter or margarine
1 green pepper, deseeded and chopped
1 red pepper, deseeded and chopped
1 onion, chopped
75 g/3 oz canned sweet corn, drained
4 chicken portions, cooked
SAUCE
150 ml/¼ pint mayonnaise
2 teaspoons curry paste
2 small onions, grated
2 teaspoons finely chopped parsley
paprika

Cook the rice in plenty of boiling salted water for 15 to 20 minutes, or until the grains are tender; drain.

Meanwhile, melt the butter or margarine in a saucepan and add the chopped peppers and onion, then cook gently for 5 minutes. Add the sweet corn and continue to cook for 5 minutes. Fold the fried vegetables into the cooked rice and season to taste. Pack into a greased 1.15-litre/2-pint ring mould, leave to cool then chill thoroughly.

Meanwhile, remove the skin and any bones from the chicken and cube the flesh. Combine the mayonnaise, curry paste, grated onions, parsley and seasoning to taste. Fold in the cubed chicken meat and chill.

To serve, turn the rice ring out on to a plate and fill the centre with the chicken mixture. Dust with a little paprika and serve. SERVES 4

Creamy Curried Pasta

—— Carol Bowen ——

225 g/8 oz pasta shapes
salt and pepper
1 onion, finely chopped
4 tablespoons dry vermouth or chicken stock
150 ml/¼ pint mayonnaise
2 teaspoons mild concentrated curry paste
2 teaspoons apricot jam
2 teaspoons lemon juice
8 large sausages, cooked and thinly sliced
GARNISH
halved tomato slices
chopped parsley

Cook the pasta in boiling salted water for 12 to 15 minutes, until tender. Drain well and allow to cool.

Place the onion and vermouth or stock in a saucepan and bring to the boil. Simmer for 3 minutes, then remove from the heat and allow to cool.

Combine the onion mixture with the mayonnaise, curry paste, apricot jam, lemon juice and seasoning. Pour over the pasta and toss well to coat. Finally fold in the cooked sausages. Turn the mixture into a serving dish and garnish it with the tomatoes and parsley. Chill for 30 minutes before serving. SERVES 4

Eggs Mulligatawny

— Moya Maynard —

175 g/6 oz long-grain rice
750 ml/1¼ pint chicken stock
6 large eggs, hard boiled
SAUCE
1 (440-g/15-oz) can mulligatawny soup
1 tablespoon cornflour
1 tablespoon tomato purée
2 tablespoons sweet chutney
40 g/1½ oz sultanas
watercress sprigs to garnish

Place the rice in a saucepan with the stock, bring to the boil, then reduce the heat and simmer for 12 to 15 minutes.

To make the sauce, pour the soup into a saucepan. Blend the cornflour with a little water and add to the soup with the remaining ingredients. Bring slowly to the boil, stirring, and cook for about 5 minutes until the cornflour thickens.

Drain the rice and arrange it on a heated dish. Cut the eggs into halves lengthways and arrange on the rice. Spoon the sauce over the eggs and garnish with watercress. Serve with redcurrant jelly and salted peanuts, if liked. SERVES 4

Spaghetti alla Marinara

— Marguerite Patten —

100 g/4 oz spaghetti
salt and pepper
2 large tomatoes
50 g/2 oz mushrooms
25 g/1 oz butter or margarine
1 onion, chopped
100 g/4 oz cooked white fish, flaked
50 g/2 oz peeled prawns (optional)
a little chopped parsley
50 g/2 oz cheese, grated

Cook the spaghetti in plenty of boiling salted water until tender. Meanwhile, peel and chop the tomatoes and slice the mushrooms. Melt the butter or margarine in a frying pan, add the onion, mushrooms and tomatoes and cook gently until the onion is soft.

Add the cooked fish and prawns, if used, and season to taste. Strain the spaghetti, then add it to the fish mixture. Toss and heat for a few minutes, then add chopped parsley and grated cheese and serve immediately. SERVES 2

Bolognaise Sauce

— Jane Todd —

50 g/2 oz butter
3 rindless rashers bacon, chopped
1 onion, chopped
1 clove garlic, crushed
2 carrots, chopped
2 sticks celery, chopped
225 g/8 oz minced beef
100 g/4 oz minced pork
100 g/4 oz minced veal
1 (227-g/8-oz) can peeled tomatoes
150 ml/¼ pint chicken stock
150 ml/¼ pint red wine
2 tablespoons tomato purée
pinch of grated nutmeg
225 g/8 oz mushrooms, sliced
salt and pepper
4 tablespoons double cream

Melt the butter in a saucepan and sauté the bacon in it for 2 minutes. Add the onion, garlic, carrots and celery and sauté until the vegetables are beginning to soften. Add the meats and continue cooking, stirring, until browned on all sides. Add the tomatoes with their juice, stock, wine, tomato purée, nutmeg, mushrooms and seasoning. Bring to the boil, reduce the heat and cover the pan. Simmer for 1 hour, then stir in the cream just before serving. SERVES 6

Cheese and Mushroom Noodles

— Moya Maynard —

40 g/1½ oz butter or margarine
1 medium onion, chopped
100 g/4 oz mushrooms, washed and halved
1 (106-g/3¾-oz) packet cheese slices
175 g/6 oz ribbon noodles
salt and pepper
1 teaspoon lemon juice
chopped parsley to garnish

Melt the butter or margarine in a frying pan, add the onion and cook gently for about 10 minutes until soft. Add the mushrooms and cook for a further 2 minutes. Cut the cheese into matchstick lengths.

Meanwhile, cook the noodles in plenty of boiling salted water for about 8 minutes, or until just tender. Drain well and return the noodles to the pan. Stir in the cooked onion and mushroom mixture, the cheese, seasoning and lemon juice. Mix thoroughly and serve immediately, garnished with chopped parsley. SERVES 2

Kidney and Pasta Sauté

— Marguerite Patten —

6 lamb's kidneys
1 tablespoon seasoned plain flour
1 tablespoon oil
25 g/1 oz butter
1 small onion, sliced
3 rindless rashers bacon, chopped
1 (200-g/7-oz) can peeled tomatoes
1 tablespoon tomato purée
450 ml/¾ pint chicken stock
1 teaspoon Worcestershire sauce
1 tablespoon sherry
50 g/2 oz pasta shapes
salt and pepper
chopped parsley to garnish (optional)

Skin, halve and core the kidneys, then dust them in seasoned flour. Heat the oil and butter together in a saucepan, then add the onion and bacon and fry for 2 to 3 minutes. Add the prepared kidneys and continue cooking until the kidneys are sealed on the outside.

Stir in the tomatoes, tomato purée, chicken stock, Worcestershire sauce and sherry and bring to the boil. Add the dry pasta and salt and pepper to taste. Cover the pan and cook gently until the pasta is just tender – about 30 minutes. Lift off the lid towards the end of the cooking time if the mixture is too moist. Serve piping hot, sprinkled with a little chopped parsley if liked. SERVES 4

Veal-stuffed Cannelloni

— Jane Todd —

8 cannelloni tubes
1 tablespoon oil
FILLING
100 g/4 oz butter
50 g/2 oz mushrooms, chopped
350 g/12 oz minced veal
pinch of grated nutmeg
salt and pepper
about 6 tablespoons water
600 ml/1 pint Tomato Sauce (page 125)
grated Parmesan cheese

Cook the cannelloni in plenty of boiling salted water, with the oil added, until tender. Drain and rinse in cold water.

To make the filling, melt half the butter in a frying pan and sauté the mushrooms for 3 to 4 minutes. Stir in the minced veal, nutmeg and seasoning and continue to cook until the veal is browned. Add the water and allow the mixture to simmer for about 20 minutes, stirring occasionally to prevent it from sticking.

Allow the meat mixture to cool slightly, then use to fill the cannelloni – the easiest way to do this is to spoon the filling into a large piping bag fitted with a plain nozzle and pipe it into the cannelloni. Even so, careful handling is necessary to avoid splitting the cannelloni.

Arrange the filled cannelloni in a greased ovenproof dish and pour over the tomato sauce. Sprinkle the surface generously with grated Parmesan cheese and dot with the remaining butter. Cook, uncovered, in a moderate oven (180 C, 350 F, gas 4) for 30 to 35 minutes, until bubbling and lightly browned. SERVES 4

Lasagne Verdi

— Jane Todd —

12 sheets lasagne verdi
salt and pepper
1 tablespoon oil
Bolognaise Sauce (page 116)
600 ml/1 pint Béchamel Sauce (page 20)
50 g/2 oz cheese, grated
2 tablespoons grated Parmesan cheese

Bring a pan of salted water to the boil, add the lasagne with the oil and cook until just tender. Drain and rinse in cold water. Lay the sheets of lasagne on absorbent kitchen paper to dry. Meanwhile, make the Bolognaise Sauce and the Béchamel Sauce.

To assemble the lasagne, line the base of a lightly greased ovenproof dish with some of the lasagne. Spread with a layer of bolognaise sauce followed by a layer of béchamel sauce. Continue in this way, ending with a layer of béchamel sauce on top. Sprinkle the surface with a mixture of the cheeses and cook in a moderately hot oven (200 C, 400 F, gas 6) for 40 to 45 minutes, until browned and bubbling. Or cool, cover with cling film and store in the refrigerator until ready to cook. Serve with a tossed green salad. SERVES 4

Fondue Cookery

What better way to entertain friends than to gather round for a delicious fondue? Not only is this a simple, fun way of entertaining, but it can be quite economical too.

Mixed Fondue with Peppered Tomato Sauce, Curried Mayonnaise, Deviled Mayonnaise and Yogurt Herb Sauce

Mixed Fondue

To prepare a mixed fondue, serve a selection of foods which can be deep fried. For example, offer fine slices of frying steak, sliced smoked sausage, small meatballs about the size of walnuts, thin slices of chicken breast, small bacon rolls and some fish – peeled cooked prawns, small chunks of white fish or fishballs.

Arrange the chosen foods on platters or piled in dishes and garnish them with herbs, lemons and tomatoes – it is important to make the raw food look attractive. Serve a selection of sauces to accompany the cooked food, a salad and some bread. Garlic bread can also be served, if you like. Prepare a small amount of batter which can be used to coat the fish pieces before they are cooked.

Heat enough oil to two-thirds fill the fondue pan – do this on the hob before you serve the fondue. Transfer the pan to the burner and keep the oil hot enough to cook the food. Guests help themselves to foods, spearing each piece with a fondue fork and dipping it in the hot oil (or in batter first, if necessary) until cooked. If the oil cools during the meal, quickly reheat it on the hob before any more items are cooked.

Choose from the following sauces, or serve bottled chutneys and relishes if you prefer.

Yogurt Herb Sauce Mix plenty of chopped fresh herbs, seasoning and about 50 g/2 oz cream cheese with 150 ml/$\frac{1}{4}$ pint natural yogurt. Chill lightly before serving.

Devilled Mayonnaise Mix $\frac{1}{4}$ teaspoon chilli powder, $\frac{1}{2}$ teaspoon Worcestershire sauce, 2 tablespoons tomato purée and 1 tablespoon grated onion into 300 ml/$\frac{1}{2}$ pint mayonnaise. Add seasoning to taste and chill thoroughly. Serve sprinkled with a little extra chilli powder or paprika if you prefer.

Curried Mayonnaise Stir 1 tablespoon concentrated curry paste, 1 tablespoon grated onion, 2 finely chopped green chillies and the grated rind of 1 small lemon into 300 ml/$\frac{1}{2}$ pint mayonnaise. Chill thoroughly and serve garnished with a little chopped fresh coriander and a couple of small whole red or green chillies.

Peppered Tomato Sauce Finely chop 1 large onion and 2 green or red deseeded peppers. Fry these in a little butter until soft but not browned. Add 1 (425-g/15-oz) can tomatoes and bring to the boil. Cover and simmer for 5 minutes, then taste and adjust the seasoning and stir in 2 tablespoons chopped parsley and a little paprika. Serve immediately.

Sauces for Fish Fondues

— Diana Jaggar —

Avocado Sauce Mash a ripe avocado pear with a little lemon juice and some French dressing. Add a little mayonnaise, double cream, Worcestershire sauce, diced cucumber and seasoning to taste.

Tomato Chilli Sauce Mix together mayonnaise, tomato chutney, finely grated onion, 1–2 teaspoons Tabasco, lemon juice, salt and pepper and whipped cream.

Hollandaise Sauce

— Marguerite Patten —

2 egg yolks
pinch of cayenne pepper
salt and pepper
1-2 tablespoons lemon juice or white
wine vinegar
25-50 g/2-4 oz butter

Place the egg yolks and cayenne in a bowl with the seasoning and lemon juice or vinegar. Place the bowl over a pan of hot, not boiling, water and whisk until the sauce begins to thicken. Add the butter in very small pieces, whisking in each piece until completely melted before adding the next. Do not allow to boil or the sauce will curdle. If the sauce is too thick, add a little cream.
SERVES 4

Crispy Fried Fish Balls

Jill Spencer

50 g/2 oz butter · 50 g/2 oz plain flour
150 ml/¼ pint milk
350 g/12 oz smoked haddock fillet, cooked,
skinned and flaked
grated rind of ½ lemon
salt and pepper
1 tablespoon chopped parsley
2 hard-boiled eggs, chopped
COATING
1 egg, beaten · breadcrumbs for coating
oil for deep frying

Place the butter, flour and milk in a liquidiser and switch on to maximum speed for 30 seconds. Pour into a saucepan and bring to the boil, whisking all the time. Simmer the sauce over a low heat for 1 minute. Stir in the remaining ingredients, making sure there are no bones in the fish, and spread the mixture in a shallow dish. Mark into 12 portions and chill until firm enough to handle.

Roll the portions into balls, using a little flour if necessary, then dip them in the beaten egg and coat them in breadcrumbs. Heat the oil to 180c/350f in a suitable fondue pan. Cook the fish balls at the table and serve a Tomato Sauce (page 125) as an accompaniment. SERVES 4

Fried Fish Fondue

Diana Jaggar

225 g/8 oz haddock or cod fillet, cooked
40 g/1½ oz butter · 40 g/1½ oz plain flour
150 ml/¼ pint milk
3 tablespoons double cream
a little lemon juice
salt and cayenne pepper
1 egg, beaten · breadcrumbs for coating
450 g/1 lb whitebait, washed
450 g/1 lb unpeeled prawns
225 g/8 oz whole button mushrooms, washed

For the fish balls, flake the haddock or cod, removing all the skin and bones. Melt the butter in a small saucepan and stir in the flour. Gradually pour in the milk and bring to the boil, stirring continuously, to make a thick sauce. Remove the pan from the heat and stir in the cream and flaked fish. Add a little lemon juice and seasoning to taste, then beat well. Allow to cool and chill thoroughly.

Shape spoonfuls of the fish mixture into walnut-sized balls (flour your hands first). Coat the fish balls in beaten egg and then in breadcrumbs. Arrange these on individual plates with the whitebait, prawns and mushrooms. Each guest spears a piece of fish and cooks it in the hot oil in the fondue pan.

Serve cooked rice, a fresh salad, the Avocado Sauce and Tomato Chilli Sauce (both opposite) to accompany the fish. SERVES 4

Fondue Bourguignonne

Jill Spencer

575 g/1¼ lb fillet or rump steak
oil for deep frying

Cut the beef into small cubes. Heat the oil in the fondue pan over a gentle heat. The oil should not come more than half way up the sides of the pan. When the oil is hot enough, a cube of day-old bread should turn golden brown within one minute of cooking.

Arrange the meat on individual plates; each person spears a piece and cooks it to taste in the hot oil. Serve baked potatoes, salads and French bread to accompany the fondue with the sauces. SERVES 4

Cucumber and Soured Cream Sauce Peel and dice half a cucumber, then mix it with 150 ml/¼ pint soured cream, 4 tablespoons mayonnaise, 1 tablespoon chopped chives and seasoning to taste. Chill lightly before serving.

Tomato Sauce Finely chop 1 large onion and sauté it in 50 g/2 oz butter until soft but not browned. Add a bay leaf, salt and pepper, 1 teaspoon oregano and 1 tablespoon plain flour. Cook for a minute, then stir in 2 (425-g/15-oz) cans tomatoes and 2 tablespoons tomato purée. Simmer for 20 minutes, remove the bay leaf and blend in a liquidiser before serving.

Bacon and Corn Fondue

Jill Spencer

150 ml/¼ pint dry white wine
450 g/1 lb Swiss cheese, grated
2 teaspoons cornflour
100 g/4 oz canned sweet corn, drained
75 g/3 oz rindless rashers lean bacon, chopped
and fried
1 tablespoon chopped parsley
freshly ground black pepper

Pour most of the wine into a fondue pan and heat gently. Gradually stir in the cheese and cook gently, stirring continuously, until smooth and melted.

Blend the cornflour with the remaining wine until smooth and stir into the fondue with the sweet corn, bacon, parsley and pepper to taste. Serve cubes of French bread to dip in the fondue. SERVES 3 TO 4

Spicy Meatballs

Jill Spencer

1 onion, finely chopped
1 tablespoon oil
450 g/1 lb minced beef
salt and pepper
¼ teaspoon grated nutmeg
¼ teaspoon garlic salt
1 egg, beaten
cooking oil

Sauté the onion in the hot oil until soft – about 5 to 10 minutes. Mix it with the minced beef, seasoning, nutmeg, garlic salt and beaten egg. Using floured hands, shape the meat mixture into walnut-sized balls. Arrange the meatballs on individual plates.

Pour enough oil into the fondue pan to half fill it, then heat it to 180 C/350 F. Guests spear the meatballs and cook them in the hot oil. Serve with Green Pepper and Gherkin Sauce (below), mustard, peach chutney and mango chutney. SERVES 4

Green Pepper and Gherkin Sauce

Jill Spencer

1 onion, chopped
2 green peppers, chopped
4 large gherkins, sliced
25 g/1 oz butter
4 tablespoons water
salt and pepper
¼ teaspoon chilli sauce

Sauté the onion, green pepper and gherkins together in the butter until golden. Add the remaining ingredients, bring to the boil and simmer for 10 minutes, stirring occasionally.

Traditional Cheese Fondue

Jill Spencer

1 clove garlic
150 ml/¼ pint dry white wine
1 teaspoon lemon juice
275 g/10 oz Emmental cheese, grated
275 g/10 oz Gruyère cheese, grated
1 tablespoon cornflour
3 tablespoons kirsch
pinch of white pepper
pinch of grated nutmeg
pinch of paprika

Rub the inside of a fondue pan with the cut clove of garlic. Pour the wine into the pan with the lemon juice and heat gently. Gradually add the cheeses, stirring continuously, and heat gently until all the cheese has melted.

When the mixture begins to bubble, blend the cornflour and kirsch together and add to the fondue. Continue to cook gently, again stirring continuously, for a further 2 to 3 minutes and season to taste with pepper, nutmeg and paprika. Serve cubes of French bread to dip in the fondue. SERVES 4

Horseradish Fondue

Jill Spencer

15 g/½ oz butter
225 g/8 oz Cheddar cheese, grated
4 tablespoons milk
1 tablespoon Worcestershire sauce
2 teaspoons dried grated horseradish
salt and pepper
1 tablespoon plain flour
1 tablespoon water
1 tablespoon dry white wine

Place the butter and cheese together in a fondue pan and allow to melt over a low heat, stirring frequently. Stir in the milk, Worcestershire sauce, horseradish and seasoning. Blend the flour with the water and stir into the fondue. When smooth and thick add the white wine and reheat, stirring all the time.

Serve artichoke hearts, cubes of cooked ham and cauliflower florets to dip in the fondue. SERVES 2

Asparagus Fondue

Jill Spencer

150 ml/¼ pint dry white wine
450 g/1 lb Swiss cheese, grated
1 tablespoon cornflour
1 (340-g/12-oz) can asparagus spears
2 tablespoons chopped parsley
freshly ground black pepper
cayenne pepper

Pour the wine into the fondue pan and heat gently. Gradually add the cheese and cornflour, mixed, and stir constantly until all the cheese has melted. Drain the asparagus and cut it into 2.5-cm/1-in lengths. Stir the asparagus into the fondue with the remaining ingredients. Use cubes of cooked ham and French bread to dip in the fondue. SERVES 4

Onion and Mushroom Fondue

Jill Spencer

50 g/2 oz butter
2 shallots, finely chopped
50 g/2 oz mushrooms, chopped
300 ml/½ pint dry white wine
350 g/12 oz Gruyère cheese, grated
350 g/12 oz Emmental cheese, grated
pinch of dry mustard
pinch of grated nutmeg
1 tablespoon cornflour
2 tablespoons kirsch
chopped parsley to garnish

Melt the butter in a fondue pan and sauté the shallots and mushrooms in it for 5 to 10 minutes. Pour in the white wine and reheat gently. Gradually add the cheeses, stirring continuously until melted. Add the mustard and nutmeg, then blend the cornflour with kirsch and stir into the fondue. Cook for a further 10 minutes, stirring all the time, until thickened. Garnish with the parsley and serve with small button mushrooms, cubes of bread and pickled onions to dip. SERVES 4 TO 6

Farmhouse Fondue

———— Jill Spencer ————

1 clove garlic
450 g/1 lb Cheddar cheese, grated
150 ml/¼ pint milk
salt and pepper
pinch of dry mustard
pinch of grated nutmeg
2 tablespoons dry white wine (optional)

Rub the inside of a fondue pan with the cut clove of garlic. Add the cheese and melt it slowly over a very gentle heat, stirring continously. Stir in the remaining ingredients. Cook until thickened and creamy, stirring all the time.

Serve cubes of French bread to dip in the fondue.
SERVES 4

Cider Fondue

———— Jill Spencer ————

450 ml/¾ pint dry cider
675 g/1½ lb Gruyère cheese, grated
2 tablespoons plain flour
3 tablespoons Calvados
salt and pepper
pinch of grated nutmeg

Heat the cider in a fondue pan. Gradually add the cheese and flour, mixed together, and heat gently until all the cheese has melted, stirring continuously.

Stir in the remaining ingredients and cook for a few minutes until the fondue has thickened. Serve quartered dessert apples (dipped in a little lemon juice to prevent discoloration) and cubes of French bread to dip in the fondue. SERVES 6

Barbecues and Picnics

Whether it's a simple barbecue in your own garden or an elaborate picnic party, outdoor eating is great fun. All the ideas you need to ensure that your summer extravaganzas are a success are here – from fantastic filled rolls to aromatic grills.

Picnic Rolls, Pork and Apple Barbecue and Seafood Kebabs

Pork and Apple Barbecue

Bridget Jones

(ILLUSTRATED ON PREVIOUS PAGE)

4 lean pork chops
2 cooking apples, cored and sliced
a little lemon juice
salt and pepper
a few sage leaves
oil for cooking
a little demerara sugar
sage sprigs to garnish

Trim any excess fat off the chops. Dip the apple slices in a little lemon juice to prevent them from discolouring. Season the chops and cook them on the barbecue with the sage leaves to give flavour. Turn the chops to cook the second side and make sure that the meat is cooked through. Brush the chops with oil during cooking, but do not make them too greasy.

When the chops are almost cooked, place the apple slices over the coals and cook until browned underneath. Turn over and sprinkle a little demerara sugar on top, then cook for a few minutes and serve these with the chops, garnished with a few fresh sage sprigs. SERVES 4

Seafood Sauce

Carol Bowen

6 tablespoons thick mayonnaise
1 tablespoon tomato purée
2 tablespoons lemon juice
1 tablespoon Worcestershire sauce
1 teaspoon grated lemon rind
1 teaspoon finely chopped onion
2 teaspoons chopped parsley
salt and pepper

Blend all the ingredients together with a wooden spoon until smooth and well mixed. Place in the refrigerator and chill for at least 1 hour before serving. SERVES 4

Tuna Steaks with Mustard

Carol Bowen

50 g/2 oz butter, melted
3 teaspoons prepared mustard
1 tablespoon lemon juice
salt and pepper
4 individual tuna or cod steaks
lemon slices to garnish

Combine the melted butter with the mustard, lemon juice and seasoning to taste. Brush half this mixture over the steaks, on both sides, then grill the fish over medium coals for 10 minutes. Turn, brush with the remaining mixture and grill for a further 10 minutes.

Serve hot, with any of the remaining mustard mixture and lemon slices to garnish. SERVES 4

Seafood Kebabs

Carol Bowen

6 rindless rashers streaky bacon
225 g/8 oz plaice fillets
salt and pepper
3 crayfish tails, peeled
8 large cooked prawns, peeled
1 large lemon, cut into 4 thick slices
MARINADE
1 lemon
150 ml/$\frac{1}{4}$ pint olive oil
1 clove garlic, crushed
$\frac{1}{4}$ teaspoon salt
bay leaf

Prepare the marinade first by carefully paring the rind from the lemon. Add the rind to the juice squeezed from the lemon, the oil, garlic, salt and bay leaf. Mix together thoroughly.

Place the bacon rashers on a board and stretch them with the back of a round-bladed knife. Cut each rasher into two. Skin the plaice fillets and divide the fish into twelve pieces. Place each piece of fish on half a bacon rasher, season and roll up, enclosing the fish completely. Secure each with a wooden cocktail stick. Cut each crayfish tail into four pieces. Place the bacon rolls, prawns and crayfish in the marinade and leave for 2 hours, turning occasionally.

Cut each lemon slice into four pieces. Remove the cocktail sticks from the bacon rolls and put them with the prawns and crayfish on four long or eight short skewers, alternating with the pieces of lemon. Cook the kebabs over medium coals for about 10 minutes, turning and brushing occasionally with the marinade. Serve with Seafood Sauce. SERVES 4

Malaysian Dindings Duck

Carol Bowen

1 tablespoon ground coriander
2 teaspoons ground fenugreek
2 teaspoons ground cumin
2 teaspoons turmeric
1 teaspoon ground cinnamon
½ teaspoon ground cardamom
¼ teaspoon ground cloves
¼ teaspoon grated nutmeg
1 teaspoon mild chilli powder
1 teaspoon freshly ground black pepper
½ teaspoon salt
1 small piece fresh root ginger, grated
juice of 1 lemon
2 small onions, minced
2 cloves garlic, crushed
100 g/4 oz desiccated coconut
250 ml/8 fl oz boiling water
1 (2.25-kg/5-lb) oven-ready duck

Mix all the spices and seasonings together in a bowl with the ginger, lemon juice, onions and garlic. Soak the coconut in the boiling water for 5 minutes, then add to the spice mixture. Stir well to make a thick paste.

Split the duck open through the breastbone and open out flat. Secure the duck flat with skewers if necessary. Spread the paste all over the duck and cook over medium coals for 1½ to 2 hours. Turn and baste occasionally. Serve with a crisp salad. SERVES 4

Honey Barbecued Chicken

Carol Bowen

50 g/2 oz butter
1 medium onion, chopped
1 clove garlic, crushed (optional)
1 (396-g/14-oz) can peeled tomatoes
2 tablespoons Worcestershire sauce
2 tablespoons honey
salt and pepper
4 large *or* 8 small chicken drumsticks
watercress sprigs to garnish

Place the butter, onion, garlic, tomatoes with their can juice, Worcestershire sauce, honey and seasoning in a small saucepan. Heat gently for 30 minutes.

Brush the drumsticks with the sauce and cook over a barbecue for 10 to 15 minutes on each side, depending upon size, brushing frequently with the sauce. Serve any remaining sauce separately with the cooked chicken, garnish with watercress and accompany with a rice and vegetable salad. SERVES 4

Minced Beef Shasliks

— *Carol Bowen* —

450 g/1 lb lean finely minced beef
1 teaspoon salt
$\frac{1}{2}$ teaspoon freshly ground black pepper
1 tablespoon grated onion
1 tablespoon Worcestershire sauce
4 large onions
8 bay leaves
oil to baste

Combine the beef, salt, pepper, grated onion and Worcestershire sauce in a bowl. Wet your hands and shape the meat into small balls about the size of a large walnut. Blanch the onions in boiling water for 2 to 3 minutes, then cut into quarters.

Thread the meatballs, onion quarters and bay leaves on to four skewers, alternating the ingredients. Brush with oil and cook over medium coals for 15 to 20 minutes, or until cooked. Serve with grilled tomatoes and a crisp salad. SERVES 4

Rolled Veal and Ham Kebabs

— *Carol Bowen* —

4 veal escalopes
4 thin slices cooked shoulder ham
1 small green pepper, deseeded
1 tablespoon French mustard
24 stuffed green olives
150 ml/$\frac{1}{4}$ pint natural yogurt
2 tablespoons lemon juice
4 tablespoons oil
salt and pepper

Place the veal escalopes between two sheets of dampened greaseproof paper. Beat out until very thin. Divide each veal escalope into four pieces. Cut each slice of ham into four pieces and the pepper into 12 pieces.

Spread each portion of veal with mustard, top with a slice of ham and roll up with the ham inside. Thread the veal rolls on to four kebab skewers, alternating with the pieces of green pepper and the olives.

Mix the yogurt, lemon juice, oil and seasoning to taste together in a small bowl. Spoon over the kebabs and allow to marinate for about 2 hours.

Cook over medium coals for 10 to 15 minutes, basting frequently with the marinade. Serve any unused marinade with the cooked kebabs. SERVES 4

Skewered Noisettes of Lamb

Carol Bowen

4 noisettes of lamb
2 teaspoons prepared mustard
1 clove garlic, chopped
few rosemary sprigs, crushed
8 shallots or small onions
8 small tomatoes
olive oil
salt and pepper

Trim the noisettes of lamb and spread each side lightly with mustard. Sprinkle with a little chopped garlic and crushed rosemary.

Peel and parboil the onions until they are almost tender. Thread the onions on to skewers with the lamb noisettes and tomatoes. Brush with oil and season with salt and pepper. Grill over medium coals for 30 minutes, turning frequently. Serve with boiled rice. SERVES 4

Holiday Burgers with Cucumber Salad

Audrey Ellis

CUCUMBER SALAD
1 cucumber, peeled
2 teaspoons salt
150 ml/$\frac{1}{4}$ pint soured cream
4 spring onions, finely chopped
BURGERS
450 g/1 lb minced beef
salt and pepper
oil for brushing
GARNISH
shredded lettuce
8 spring onions
1 small onion, sliced into rings
1 tomato, sliced · 4 gherkins

To make the cucumber salad, dice the cucumber and place it in a strainer. Sprinkle with the salt and leave for 15 to 20 minutes, then dry on absorbent kitchen paper. Place the cucumber in a serving dish, top with the soured cream and garnish with the spring onions.

Mix the minced beef with seasoning to taste and shape it into four burgers. Brush the burgers with a little oil and cook under a hot grill or over a barbecue until browned on the outside and juicy in the middle. Allow 4 to 6 minutes on each side, according to taste.

Arrange the lettuce on four plates. Place a burger on each and add two spring onions. Garnish the burgers with onion rings, slices of tomato and gherkin fans. SERVES 4

Picnic Rolls

(ILLUSTRATED ON PAGES 130/131)

Allow three finger rolls per person and fill them generously with any of the following combinations. Pack the rolls carefully in cling film or close together in a covered container. Take a jar of mayonnaise, soured cream or salad dressing along to moisten the filling just before the rolls are eaten.

Ham Salad Place a large slice of ham, rolled or folded, some tomato wedges and trimmed spring onions in each roll. Add a few sprigs of watercress or mustard and cress and a little seasoning.

Cottage Cheese and Cucumber Cup a large lettuce leaf in the split roll and fill it with cottage cheese, seasoned to taste. Arrange sliced cucumber on top and sprinkle a little chopped mint down the middle.

Egg and Cheese Half fill the rolls with grated cheese, then top with quartered hard-boiled eggs and wedges of tomato. Season to taste and add a few sprigs of parsley if you like.

Salami and Coleslaw Cup two slices of salami in each roll and fill them with a little coleslaw. Top with a couple of halved tomato slices.

Smoked Mackerel Cream Mix flaked smoked mackerel with mayonnaise, seasoning and some chopped parsley. Arrange cupped lettuce leaves in the rolls and fill with the mackerel mixture. Garnish with lemon wedges.

Prawn Cocktail Mix cooked peeled prawns with mayonnaise, a little tomato purée and seasoning to taste. Add a dash of Worcestershire sauce and spoon the mixture into cupped lettuce leaves in the rolls. Top with a couple of cooked, unpeeled prawns and parsley.

Golden Wrapped Eggs

—————— Carol Bowen ——————

350 g/12 oz pork sausagemeat
1 teaspoon dried mixed herbs
4 hard-boiled eggs, shelled
1 (368-g/13-oz) packet frozen puff pastry, defrosted
beaten egg to glaze

Mix the sausagemeat with the herbs until well blended. Divide into four portions and shape each portion around a hard-boiled egg to cover it completely.

Divide the pastry into four portions and roll each piece out, on a lightly floured surface, to a 15-cm/6-in square. Reserve any pastry trimmings. Place an egg in the centre of each square, moisten the edges of the pastry with water and wrap the pastry around the egg, completely enclosing it. Place, sealed edges down, on a dampened baking tray and decorate the tops with pastry leaves made from the reserved pastry trimmings. Make a small slit in the top of each to allow any steam to escape.

Glaze each pastry-wrapped egg with beaten egg and bake in a hot oven (220 c, 425 f, gas 7) for 25 to 35 minutes or until golden brown. Serve cold with a mixed salad. SERVES 4

Picnic Pie

—————— Carol Bowen ——————

PASTRY
275 g/10 oz wholemeal flour
salt and pepper
65 g/2½ oz margarine · 65 g/2½ oz lard
4 tablespoons cold water
FILLING
2 large chicken portions
25 g/1 oz fresh white breadcrumbs
grated rind of 1 lemon
pinch of dried thyme
1 tablespoon chopped parsley
1 large onion, chopped
3 rindless rashers lean bacon, chopped
50 g/2 oz mushrooms, chopped
4 tablespoons cold water
beaten egg to glaze

To make the pastry, place the flour in a bowl with a pinch of salt. Add the margarine and lard, cut into small pieces, and rub the fat in with the fingertips until the mixture resembles fine breadcrumbs. Add the water and mix to make a stiff dough.

Divide the pastry in half and roll out one piece on a lightly floured surface. When rolled out, the pastry should be large enough to line a deep 20-cm/8-in pie plate.

To prepare the filling, remove the skin from the chicken portions, cut the chicken flesh away from the bone and cut it into small pieces. Place the breadcrumbs in a bowl with the lemon rind, thyme and parsley. Add the chicken meat. Mix the onion, bacon and mushrooms together in another bowl.

Arrange half the onion mixture over the pastry-lined plate, season generously, cover with the chicken and breadcrumb mixture, then top with the remaining onion mixture. Season again and sprinkle with the water.

Roll out the remaining pastry until large enough to cover the pie plate. Dampen the pastry rim with water and cover with the pastry lid. Trim and flute the edges. Use any pastry trimmings to make leaves to decorate the pie. Make a small hole in the centre of the pie to allow any steam to escape. Glaze with the beaten egg.

Bake in a moderate oven (180 c, 350 f, gas 4) for about 1½ hours, until the filling is cooked. If the pastry starts to become too brown during cooking, cover the top with a piece of cooking foil. Allow to cool, then serve with a crisp, fresh salad. SERVES 6

Puff Cheese Whirls

— Audrey Ellis —

225 g/8 oz frozen puff pastry, defrosted
50 g/2 oz blue cheese
40 g/1½ oz cream cheese
1 teaspoon Worcestershire sauce
generous pinch of cayenne pepper

Roll out the pastry thinly to an oblong about 30 × 20 cm/
12 × 8 in. Crumble the blue cheese into a basin and beat in
the cream cheese, Worcestershire sauce and cayenne.
Spread this mixture evenly over the pastry and roll up
tightly starting from one long edge, like a Swiss roll. Chill
until firm.

Cut the roll into 5-mm/¼-in slices and lay these flat, and
well apart, on non-stick baking trays (or baking trays
lined with non-stick paper).

Bake in a hot oven (220 c, 425 f, gas 7) for 10 to 12
minutes, or until golden brown. Cool and remove to a wire
rack before completely cold. MAKES 20 TO 24

Chicken Liver and Bacon Triangles

— Audrey Ellis —

4 rindless rashers streaky bacon
175 g/6 oz chicken livers
salt and pepper
2 tablespoons rich gravy or stock
1 tablespoon apricot or peach chutney
450 g/1 lb frozen puff pastry, defrosted
1 egg, beaten

Finely chop the bacon and roughly chop the chicken
livers. Fry the bacon in a heavy-based frying pan until
the fat runs. Add the chicken livers, season and stir over
moderate heat until just firm. Add the gravy and chutney
and remove from the heat to cool.

Roll out the pastry thinly and cut out 12 (10-cm/4-in)
squares. Divide the filling between the pastry squares.
Brush the edges with beaten egg, fold over diagonally to
make triangular puffs and press the edges well together.
Brush the tops with the remaining beaten egg, place on a
dampened baking tray and bake in a hot oven (220 c,
425 f, gas 7) for 20 to 25 minutes, until well risen and
golden brown. Cool on a wire rack. MAKES 12

Highlander's Game Pâté

———— Audrey Ellis ————

225 g/8 oz ox liver
50 g/2 oz butter
450 g/1 lb boneless cooked hare or rabbit
4 thick rindless rashers streaky bacon
2 cloves garlic, crushed
salt and pepper
1 tablespoon fine oatmeal
2 tablespoons whisky
2 teaspoons dried rosemary
2 bay leaves

Cut the liver into large pieces. Melt the butter and use to cook the liver lightly, until just firm. Allow to cool. Mince the liver with the cooked game meat. Finely dice the bacon, or mince it with the meats for a finer texture.

Mix all the ingredients except the bay leaves (including the butter used to cook the liver) and press the mixture into a greased terrine. Smooth the surface and press the bay leaves on top of the pâté.

Cover with a lid or foil and cook in a moderate oven (180 c, 350 f, gas 4) for about 1 hour. Cool, then serve with oatcakes and butter. SERVES 4 TO 6

Anchovied Terrine of Pork

———— Audrey Ellis ————

350 g/12 oz pig's liver
350 g/12 oz belly of pork
8 canned anchovy fillets
25 g/1 oz butter
1 teaspoon anchovy oil (from the can)
50 g/2 oz onion, finely chopped
salt and pepper
1 teaspoon grated nutmeg
2 tablespoons plain flour
150 ml/$\frac{1}{4}$ pint dry white wine
2 eggs, lightly beaten
6 rindless rashers streaky bacon

Finely mince the liver, pork and anchovies. Melt the butter with the oil, and cook the onion until pale golden. Mix in the meat mixture, seasoning and nutmeg.

Blend the flour with a little wine to form a thin paste, then combine it with the eggs and remaining wine. Pour into the meat mixture and blend together well with a fork. Use the bacon to line the bases of two 20 × 10-cm/ 8 × 4-in foil dishes. Pack the meat mixture into the dishes.

Stand the containers in a bain-marie (a roasting tin half filled with warm water) and cook in a moderate oven (180 c, 350 f, gas 4) for 1$\frac{1}{2}$ hours. Remove and cool. SERVES 8 TO 10

Sausage Meatloaf in Pastry

— *Carol Bowen* —

25 g/1 oz butter
1 large onion, chopped
450 g/1 lb rindless streaky bacon
175 g/6 oz fresh white breadcrumbs
50 g/2 oz shredded beef suet
1 tablespoon chopped parsley
salt and pepper
1 egg, beaten
350 g/12 oz pork sausagemeat
175 g/6 oz cooked chicken meat, sliced
1 (368-g/13-oz) packet frozen puff pastry,
defrosted
beaten egg to glaze

Melt the butter in a saucepan and fry the onion until it is soft, about 5 minutes. Reserve eight of the bacon rashers, then chop the rest quite finely. Add to the onion and cook for a further 5 minutes. Place the breadcrumbs in a bowl and add the suet, parsley, bacon and onion mixture and seasoning to taste. Bind together with the egg.

Stretch the reserved bacon rashers with the back of a knife and use six to line the base and sides of a 1-kg/2-lb loaf tin. Spread half the sausagemeat on the base of the tin and cover with half the sliced chicken. Top with the bacon mixture, the remaining chicken and remaining sausagemeat. Lay the remaining two bacon rashers on top, cover with foil and stand the tin in a bain-marie (a roasting tin half filled with warm water). Bake in a moderate oven (180 c, 350 f, gas 4) for 1½ hours. Allow to cool, then turn the meatloaf out of its tin.

Roll out the pastry on a lightly floured surface to give a rectangle large enough to enclose the meatloaf. Brush with a little of the beaten egg. Place the cooled meatloaf on the pastry, then fold the dough to enclose it completely in a neat package. Trim and seal the edges, reserving any pastry trimmings. Glaze the pastry again with beaten egg and decorate with the pastry trimmings.

Place on a dampened baking tray and bake in a hot oven (220 c, 425 f, gas 7) for 35 to 40 minutes, until golden brown and well risen. Cool and serve sliced with a selection of salads. SERVES 8

Bacon and Sage Plait

— *Carol Bowen* —

40 g/1½ oz butter or margarine
2 onions, chopped
225 g/8 oz rindless gammon or collar bacon,
cut into 5-mm/¼-in pieces
100 g/4 oz mushrooms, thinly sliced
225 g/8 oz pork sausagemeat
1 egg, beaten
½ teaspoon dried thyme
1 tablespoon chopped parsley
2 teaspoons chopped chives
1 teaspoon chopped fresh sage
salt and pepper
1 (368-g/13-oz) packet frozen puff pastry,
defrosted
beaten egg to glaze
watercress sprigs to garnish

Melt the butter or margarine in a saucepan. Add the onions and cook for 5 minutes. Add the bacon and fry gently for 10 minutes. Stir in the mushrooms and continue cooking for a further 5 minutes. Transfer to a bowl and mix in the sausagemeat, egg, herbs and seasoning.

Roll out the pastry on a lightly floured surface to an oblong approximately 30 × 20 cm/12 × 8 in. Fold in half lengthways and make diagonal cuts 5 cm/2 in. in from the joined long edge of the pastry. Place on a dampened baking tray and open out the pastry. Spoon the prepared filling in a roll shape down the length of the pastry. Fold over the pastry strips in a lattice design and secure together with a little beaten egg. Glaze the top with the beaten egg and bake in a hot oven (220 c, 425 f, gas 7) for 30 to 40 minutes until cooked, crisp and golden. Serve garnished with watercress sprigs. SERVES 4 TO 6

Hot Puddings

Why not round off a light meal with a perfect steamed pudding or a full-flavoured fruit pie for a change? Look through the following pages and you will find recipes for all your old favourite puddings along with some heart-warming new ones.

Pears in Red Wine, Nutty Fruit Crumble and Upside-down Pudding

Nutty Fruit Crumble

— Bridget Jones —

(ILLUSTRATED ON PREVIOUS PAGE)

about 1 kg/2 lb fresh fruit – for example,
apples, blackberries, blackcurrants,
gooseberries, plums or rhubarb
sugar
TOPPING
100 g/4 oz plain flour
50 g/2 oz butter
50 g/2 oz sugar
100 g/4 oz chopped walnuts or hazelnuts

Prepare the fruit according to its type; mix two or three different types if you like. For example, mix apples with blackberries, rhubarb with sliced bananas, plums with a little orange rind. Lay the prepared fruit in an ovenproof dish and sprinkle with sugar to taste.

Sift the flour into a bowl and rub in the butter until the mixture resembles fine breadcrumbs. Stir in the sugar and nuts and sprinkle this mixture over the fruit.

Cook in a moderately hot oven (190 C, 375 F, gas 5) for about 45 minutes, or until the topping is brown and the fruit is cooked through. Serve with custard or cream. SERVES 4 TO 6

Pears in Red Wine

— Bridget Jones —

(ILLUSTRATED ON PREVIOUS PAGE)

8 firm pears
juice of 1 lemon
1 bottle red wine
1 cinnamon stick
4 cloves
75 g/3 oz sugar
pared rind of 1 orange

Peel the pears but leave their stalks in place. Brush the fruit with lemon juice to prevent it from discolouring. Pour the wine into a large saucepan and add the remaining ingredients together with the pears.

Gradually heat the wine to simmering point. Cook gently, basting the pears all the time and turning them over once or twice to make sure that they cook. When the pears are soft, remove them from the pan and arrange them in a serving dish or individual dishes.

Boil the wine until it is reduced to a thick syrupy glaze, then spoon it over the pears and serve immediately with clotted or whipped cream. SERVES 4

Upside-down Pudding

— Bridget Jones —

(ILLUSTRATED ON PREVIOUS PAGE)

fresh or canned fruit – for example pineapple
rings, cherries, bananas, pears or plums
100 g/4 oz butter or margarine
100 g/4 oz caster sugar
2 eggs
100 g/4 oz self-raising flour

Grease a 23-cm/9-in deep cake tin or straight-sided baking dish with butter and arrange the chosen fruit in the base, in a decorative pattern.

Cream the butter or margarine with the sugar until light and fluffy. Gradually beat in the eggs and fold in the flour. Spoon this mixture over the fruit and bake in a moderate oven (180 C, 350 F, gas 4) for about 1 hour. To serve, ease a knife around the side of the cake to free it from the container, then turn out on to a serving plate or dish. Serve with whipped cream or custard. SERVES 6

Christmas Pudding

— Carol Bowen —

150 g/5 oz fresh wholewheat breadcrumbs
100 g/4 oz plain flour
100 g/4 oz sultanas
100 g/4 oz seedless raisins
150 g/5 oz currants
100 g/4 oz shredded suet
65 g/2½ oz chopped mixed peel
65 g/2½ oz glacé cherries
100 g/4 oz demerara sugar
1 small cooking apple, peeled, cored and grated
40 g/1½ oz blanched almonds, chopped
pinch of grated nutmeg
1 teaspoon black treacle
2 large eggs, beaten
200 ml/7 fl oz brown ale
50 ml/2 fl oz brandy

Grease a 1.15-litre/2-pint pudding basin. Thoroughly mix all the ingredients together in a large mixing bowl. Place the mixture in the prepared basin, smooth it down and level off the top. Cover with greased greaseproof paper and a piece of greased cooking foil, pleated to allow for expansion. Secure with string. Steam the pudding steadily for 6 hours, cool and store in a damp-free place.

To serve, steam for a further 3 hours, then turn out on to a serving plate. Flame with extra brandy and accompany with brandy butter. SERVES 6 TO 8

Sussex Pond Pudding

— Carol Bowen —

225 g/8 oz self-raising flour
1 teaspoon salt
75 g/3 oz shredded suet
50 g/2 oz caster sugar
50 g/2 oz currants
about 150 ml/¼ pint water
FILLING
225 g/8 oz butter
50 g/2 oz mixed dried fruit
50 g/2 oz chopped mixed peel
100 g/4 oz glacé cherries
2 tablespoons mincemeat
1 eating apple, peeled, cored and coarsely grated

Mix the flour, salt, suet, sugar and currants together. Add the water and mix to a soft dough. Knead on a lightly floured work surface until smooth. Divide in half and roll out each piece to a 15-cm/6-in circle.

To make the filling, cream the butter and add the dried fruit, peel, cherries, mincemeat and apple. Chill lightly, then form into a ball. Place the mixture in the centre of one round, dampen the edge, cover with the second circle of dough and pinch the two edges together. Enclose in a piece of greased cooking foil and secure with string. Steam in a steamer or on a trivet in a saucepan half full of water for 2½ to 3 hours. Remove the cooking foil and serve on a warmed dish. SERVES 4

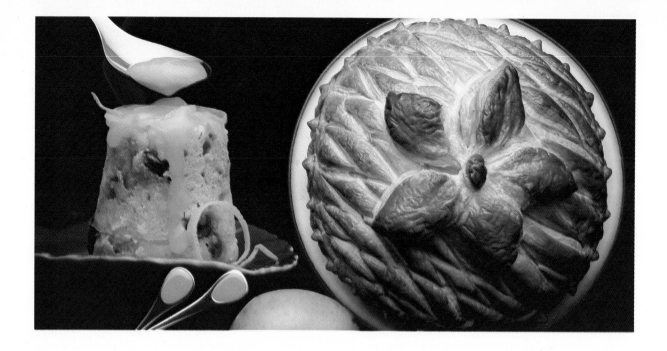

Lemon Sultana Pudding

— Audrey Ellis —

100 g/4 oz self-raising flour
pinch of salt
50 g/2 oz shredded suet
25 g/1 oz caster sugar
50 g/2 oz sultanas
grated rind and juice of 1 lemon
1 egg
3 tablespoons milk
4 tablespoons lemon curd
pared lemon rind to decorate

Sift the flour and salt into a bowl and stir in the suet, sugar, sultanas and lemon rind. Beat the egg, lemon juice and milk together, add to the dry ingredients and mix to give a soft dropping consistency. Divide between six greased dariole moulds, cover with greased foil and steam for 30 minutes.

Warm the lemon curd and add a very little boiling water to give a thin pouring sauce. Turn out the puddings, spoon a little of the lemon curd sauce over each one and decorate with strips of pared lemon rind.
SERVES 6

Yorkshire Apple Pie

— Audrey Ellis —

450 g/1 lb frozen puff pastry, defrosted
675 g/1½ lb cooking apples
175 g/6 oz Cheddar cheese, diced
50 g/2 oz seedless raisins
2–3 tablespoons soft brown sugar
grated rind and juice of ½ lemon
1 egg, beaten

Roll out the pastry and cut out two 23-cm/9-in circles. Place one circle of pastry on a dampened baking sheet.

Peel, core and slice the apples and arrange them on the pastry base, leaving a border 1 cm/½ in all round. Place the cheese and raisins on the apple and sprinkle with the sugar, lemon rind and juice. Brush the exposed pastry edges with beaten egg, place the remaining pastry circle on top and seal the edges together well. Brush the pie with beaten egg and use any pastry trimmings to decorate. Brush again with egg to glaze. Score the top surface of the pastry lightly with a sharp knife, but do not cut a steam vent.

Bake in a moderately hot oven (200 C, 400 F, gas 6) for about 40 minutes, until well risen and golden brown.
SERVES 6

Grand Marnier Soufflé

Diana Jaggar

generous 75 g/3 oz caster sugar
sponge finger biscuits or sponge cake
6 tablespoons Grand Marnier
150 ml/¼ pint milk
finely grated rind of ½ lemon
thinly pared rind of 1 orange
25 g/1 oz butter
25 g/1 oz plain flour
3 eggs, separated
a little icing sugar

Dust a greased soufflé dish with some sugar. Line with sponge fingers soaked in one third of the liqueur. Bring the milk, sugar, lemon and orange rinds to the boil. Set aside for 10 minutes. Melt the butter in a saucepan, add the flour and cook for 1 minute. Add the strained milk. Bring slowly to the boil, beating continuously until smooth. Cool, then beat in the egg yolks and remaining liqueur.

Whisk the egg whites until stiff; stir 1 tablespoon into the sauce and fold in the rest. Turn into the dish. Bake in a moderate oven (180 c, 350 f, gas 4) for 40 to 45 minutes. Dust the top of the soufflé with icing sugar, then cook for a few more minutes. Serve immediately. SERVES 4 TO 6

Normandy Apple Pie

Diana Jaggar

2 egg yolks
100 g/4 oz caster sugar
40 g/1½ oz butter
50 g/2 oz lard
2 tablespoons water
225 g/8 oz plain flour, sifted
¾ teaspoon cinnamon
50 g/2 oz walnuts, finely ground
0.5–0.75 kg/1–1½ lb Cox's apples, peeled,
cored and quartered
150 ml/¼ pint double cream, lightly whipped
caster sugar for dusting

Cream together the egg yolks, sugar, butter, lard and water. Gradually add the flour, cinnamon and walnuts to make a paste. Knead, then chill for 30 minutes. Roll out two thirds of the pastry and use to line a 20-cm/8-in fluted flan ring. Arrange the prepared apples, core side down, in the flan case. Roll out the remaining pastry to make a lid. Dampen the edges, lift the lid into position and press together. Cut a 7.5-cm/3-in circle out of the centre of the lid. Brush the pastry with cold water and dust with caster sugar. Bake in a moderate oven (180 c, 350 f, gas 4) for 35 to 40 minutes until crisp. Serve with piped whipped cream. SERVES 6

Bread and Butter Pudding

— *Carol Bowen* —

40 g/1½ oz butter, softened
8 large slices bread, crusts removed
50 g/2 oz currants
50 g/2 oz sultanas
600 ml/1 pint milk
50 g/2 oz caster sugar
2 eggs
2–3 drops vanilla essence
a little grated nutmeg
2 tablespoons demerara sugar

Butter each slice of bread on both sides and cut into four triangles. Place a layer of bread in the bottom of a 1.4-litre/2½-pint ovenproof dish. Sprinkle with half the currants and sultanas. Top with the remaining bread triangles and dried fruit.

Heat the milk with the sugar in a saucepan until dissolved. Beat the eggs with the vanilla essence in a small bowl. Pour the milk on to the egg mixture and whisk until well mixed. Strain through a fine sieve over the bread and fruit mixture and leave to soak for 10 to 15 minutes. Sprinkle with nutmeg, then bake in a moderate oven (180 c, 350 f, gas 4) for 1½ hours, until just set and golden. Sprinkle with the demerara sugar before serving. SERVES 4 TO 6

Apple Charlotte

— *Carol Bowen* —

10 slices white bread
65 g/2½ oz butter
¼ teaspoon cinnamon
50 g/2 oz dark soft brown sugar
575 g/1¼ lb cooking apples, peeled, cored and
thinly sliced
juice of 1 lemon

Trim and reserve the crusts from the bread. Lightly butter the trimmed bread slices with 40 g/1½ oz of the butter. Line a 900-ml/1½-pint ovenproof pudding basin with the bread slices, buttered side inwards, reserving a few bread slices for the lid.

Make breadcrumbs from the reserved crusts, then weigh out 50 g/2 oz of crumbs. Melt the remaining butter in a small saucepan. Add the crumbs and cook until golden. Stir in the cinnamon and sugar. Allow to cool.

Toss the apples in the lemon juice to prevent discoloration, then layer them in the basin with the breadcrumbs. Cover with the reserved bread slices, buttered side up. Cover with cooking foil and secure with string. Bake in a moderately hot oven (200 c, 400 f, gas 6) for about 1¼ hours. Allow to cool a little before turning out on to a warmed serving dish or serving it straight from the basin. Serve with cream or custard. SERVES 4

Apple Fritters

—— Carol Bowen ——

4 large dessert apples, peeled, cored and cut into
5-mm/¼-in thick rings
100 g/4 oz vanilla sugar
FRITTER BATTER
100 g/4 oz plain flour
¼ teaspoon salt
1 tablespoon oil
1 egg, separated
150 ml/¼ pint milk or milk and water
oil for deep frying
icing sugar to sprinkle

Dip the apple rings in vanilla sugar and leave to dry
slightly on absorbent kitchen paper.

Prepare the fritter batter by sifting the flour and salt
together into a bowl. Make a well in the centre and pour
in the oil and egg yolk. Gradually draw the flour into the
egg, adding the milk a little at a time, beating to produce a
smooth batter. Whisk the egg white until it stands in firm
peaks and fold into the batter mixture.

Heat the oil to 190 C/375 F and coat the apple rings in
the batter. Fry the apple rings in the oil for about 4
minutes or until golden and cooked through. Drain on
absorbent kitchen paper. Sprinkle with icing sugar and
serve. SERVES 4

Apple and Pear Dumplings

—— Carol Bowen ——

2 dessert apples
2 dessert pears
350 g/12 oz Shortcrust Pastry (page 87)
4 tablespoons mixed dried fruit
1 tablespoon clear honey
2 tablespoons chopped mixed nuts
beaten egg or milk to glaze

Grease a baking tray. Peel and core the apples and pears,
leaving the fruit whole.

Roll out the pastry on a lightly floured board or work
surface and cut out two circles of dough slightly larger
than the apples. Cut the remaining pastry into 2.5-cm/
1-in wide strips.

Mix the dried fruit, honey and nuts together in a bowl.
Place each apple on a circle of dough and fill the centres
with half of the fruit mixture. Carefully fold the pastry
around the apples, securing the dough together by
dampening the edges with a little water. Place seam side
down on the baking tray.

Fill the centres of the pears with the remaining fruit
mixture. Dampen the pastry strips with water, then
carefully wind them around the pears to enclose them
completely. Place upright on the baking tray. Use any
pastry trimmings to make decorative leaves for the apples
and pears. Glaze with beaten egg or milk and bake in a
moderately hot oven (200 C, 400 F, gas 6) for 35 to 40
minutes or until golden. Serve with pouring custard or
cream. SERVES 4

Almond Apples

Marguerite Patten

4 medium cooking apples
50 g/2 oz blanched almonds
75 g/3 oz sugar
2 egg yolks
50 g/2 oz fresh white breadcrumbs
25 g/1 oz cornflour
25 g/1 oz butter

Peel and core the apples. Chop the almonds and mix with half the sugar. Beat the egg yolks with the rest of the sugar and stir in 25 g/1 oz of the breadcrumbs. Coat the apples with this mixture.

Put the cornflour on a plate or in a paper bag and roll the apples in this; use two spoons if the cornflour is on a plate. Melt the butter in an ovenproof dish, arrange the apples in the dish and fill the centres with the almond and sugar mixture. Sprinkle with the remaining 25 g/1 oz breadcrumbs, and bake in the centre of a moderate oven (180 c, 350 f, gas 4) until tender, about 45 minutes. SERVES 4

Stacked Pancakes

Marguerite Patten

1 quantity pancake batter
FILLING
lemon curd
TOPPING
1 egg white
50 g/2 oz caster sugar
15 g/½ oz blanched almonds

Make the pancake batter. Cook just enough batter at a time in a lightly greased, hot frying pan to make thin pancakes. As they are cooked, pile the pancakes in a folded napkin to keep warm. Sandwich the cooked pancakes together with lemon curd.

To make the meringue topping, whisk the egg white until very stiff. Very gradually, beat in a little of the sugar, then fold in the remainder of the sugar. Spread the meringue over the top of the pile of filled pancakes. Decorate with almonds, then put in a very hot oven (240 c, 475 f, gas 9) for 1 to 2 minutes only, or until the meringue is lightly browned. Serve warm. SERVES 4 TO 6

Pancake Batter

Marguerite Patten

100 g/4 oz flour
pinch of salt
2 eggs
scant 300 ml/½ pint milk or milk and water
1 tablespoon olive oil

Sift the flour and salt into a bowl. Add the eggs and enough liquid to give a sticky consistency. Beat well, then gradually add the rest of the liquid, beating all the time. Add the oil last.

Crêpes Suzette

Jill Spencer

1 quantity Pancake Batter
oil for frying
4 sugar lumps
1 orange
25 g/1 oz butter
2 tablespoons sugar
1 tablespoon orange juice
1 tablespoon Curaçao
2–3 tablespoons brandy

Make the pancake batter. Brush the base of a small heavy-based frying pan with oil. Allow the oil to become hot, then pour in sufficient batter to thinly cover the pan base, tilting the pan for even spreading. Cook the pancakes for 1 to 2 minutes, then turn over to cook the other side.

Rub the sugar lumps over the orange skin to remove the zest. Crush the sugar lumps and mix them with the butter, sugar, orange juice and Curaçao.

Place the orange-flavoured butter in a heavy-based frying pan or chafing dish and allow it to melt. Fold the pancakes into four and place them, overlapped, in the pan. Baste with the butter sauce and heat through.

Pour over the brandy, allow to become warm, then ignite. When the flames have subsided, sprinkle with blanched, grated orange rind and serve immediately. SERVES 4

Orange and Almond Pudding

Audrey Ellis

100 g/4 oz soft margarine
100 g/4 oz caster sugar
2 eggs, beaten
grated rind and juice of 1 orange
100 g/4 oz self-raising flour, sifted
50 g/2 oz ground almonds
orange slices to decorate (optional)
SAUCE
2 teaspoons cornflour
300 ml/½ pint orange juice
1 tablespoon golden syrup

Cream the margarine and sugar together until soft and light. Gradually beat in the eggs and orange rind and juice, then fold in the flour and almonds. Pour the mixture into a greased 1.15-litre/2-pint pudding basin, cover with greased foil and steam over a pan of simmering water for 1½ hours.

Meanwhile, make the sauce. Moisten the cornflour with a little of the orange juice. Place the remaining juice in a saucepan with the syrup and bring to boiling point. Add the moistened cornflour and bring back to the boil, stirring constantly. Simmer for 2 minutes and serve poured over the pudding. Decorate with orange slices, if you like. SERVES 4

Rice Pudding

Marguerite Patten

50–75 g/2–3 oz round-grain rice
600 ml/1 pint milk
25–50 g/1–2 oz sugar
a little butter (optional)

Wash the rice, put it into an ovenproof pie dish and cover with the milk. Add the sugar. Cook for at least 2 hours in a cool oven (140 C, 275 F, gas 1), stirring once after the first 30 minutes. The larger quantity of rice gives a much more solid pudding.

If you are in a great hurry, you can cook the milk pudding for a shorter time at a higher temperature but the flavour is not as good.

Just before serving, stir in the butter, if used. SERVES 4

Cool Desserts

Here is a chapter full of recipes to wreck all intentions of a diet: light, fruity fools, unusual flans, glorious cheesecakes and luscious ices. For when you're feeling really adventurous there is even a recipe for a Frozen Christmas Pudding.

Fresh Fruit Salad, Raspberry Fool and Caramelised Oranges

Fresh Fruit Salad

— Bridget Jones —

(ILLUSTRATED ON PREVIOUS PAGE)

a selection of fresh fruit – for example, apples,
bananas, melon, kiwi fruit, oranges,
strawberries, grapes, pineapple and peaches
lemon juice
100 g/4 oz sugar
generous 150 ml/¼ pint water

Prepare the fruit according to its type. Slice or cube the
fruit as appropriate. Sprinkle any pieces which may
discolour with lemon juice.

Place the sugar and water in a saucepan and heat
gently, stirring continuously, until the syrup boils. Cook
for a few minutes, then pour the syrup over the fruit,
allow to cool and chill thoroughly. Serve with whipped
cream.

Caramelised Oranges

— Bridget Jones —

(ILLUSTRATED ON PREVIOUS PAGE)

225 g/8 oz sugar
100 ml/4 fl oz water
8 oranges

Place the sugar and water in a saucepan. Heat slowly,
stirring continuously until the sugar dissolves, then
bring to the boil and cook until the syrup has reduced
and caramelised.

Meanwhile, prepare the oranges: cut off all the peel (do
not discard it) and pith and slice the fruit. Remove any
pips and reshape the oranges on a heatproof serving dish
or arrange the slices in a bowl. Cut a little of the rind into
long fine threads and cook these in water until soft, then
arrange them over the fruit.

When the caramel is golden, pour it over the fruit. Take
care not to let the sugar overcook or it will become bitter.
Chill for several hours or overnight. Serve with whipped
cream. SERVES 4

Raspberry Fool

— Bridget Jones —

(ILLUSTRATED ON PREVIOUS PAGE)

450 g/1 lb raspberries
100 g/4 oz sugar
300 ml/½ pint double cream
a few whole raspberries to decorate

Place the fruit in a saucepan with the sugar and heat
gently until the juice runs. Cook for 15 minutes, then
purée the fruit in a liquidiser and press it through a fine
sieve to remove all the seeds. Leave to cool completely.

Whip the cream until stiff, then carefully fold in the
raspberry purée. Swirl the fool in individual glasses and
chill thoroughly. Decorate with a few whole raspberries
and serve with delicate biscuits. SERVES 4

Vacherin Chantilly Glacé

— Diana Jaggar —

100 g/4 oz granulated sugar
300 ml/½ pint water
pared rind and juice of 1 lemon
225 g/8 oz strawberries
50 g/2 oz icing sugar
juice of 1 large orange
6 egg whites
275 g/10 oz caster sugar
whipped cream and fresh strawberries to
decorate

Simmer the granulated sugar, water and lemon rind for
5 minutes. Cool and strain. Blend the strawberries with
the icing sugar in a liquidiser, sieve, then add the orange
and lemon juices and sugar syrup. Freeze in a shallow
container. When half frozen, beat well, then whisk one
egg white until stiff and fold into the sorbet. Freeze until
hard.

Whisk the remaining egg whites until stiff. Add 50 g/
2 oz of the caster sugar and whisk hard for 3½ minutes.
Fold in the remaining sugar. Reserve a quarter of the
meringue in the refrigerator and, using a large star nozzle,
pipe about two-thirds of the remainder into a 20-cm/8-in
circle on a baking sheet lined with non-stick paper. Pipe
the remaining one-third into a second, wide border round
the edge of the circle. Cook in a very cool oven (110c,
225 F, gas ¼) until slightly coloured – about 2 hours. Pipe
the reserved meringue on top of the second border while
the case is still hot. Return to the oven for a further 1 hour
to dry. When cool, pile the sorbet into the meringue case;
decorate and serve. SERVES 6

Caramel Oranges with Cointreau

Diana Jaggar

6 large seedless oranges
350 g/12 oz sugar · 300 ml/½ pint water
3 tablespoon Cointreau
CARAMEL
175 g/6 oz sugar · 4 tablespoons water

Pare the rind thinly from four of the oranges and cut it into long julienne strips. Blanch the rind for 15 minutes, drain and rinse it in cold water. Bring the sugar and water to the boil, add the orange strips and simmer them for 30 minutes. Add the Cointreau and set aside to cool.

Cut away all the remaining skin and pith from the oranges. Slice each orange thinly and reshape, holding the fruit together with a cocktail stick. Strain the syrup over the oranges, reserving the orange strips. Chill.

Meanwhile, make the caramel by dissolving the sugar in the water. Cook steadily to a rich brown colour, without stirring. Pour immediately on to a well-oiled surface or waxed paper. Leave to harden, then crush in a mortar or with a rolling pin. Sprinkle over the oranges, with the reserved strips of rind. SERVES 6

Fresh Peach and Almond Flan

Diana Jaggar

100 g/4 oz butter
100 g/4 oz caster sugar
grated rind of 1½ lemons
1 small egg plus 1 yolk
175 g/6 oz plain flour, sifted
100 g/4 oz ground almonds
3 large ripe peaches, halved
175 g/6 oz granulated sugar, dissolved
in 300 ml/½ pint water
175 g/6 oz cream cheese
2 tablespoons single cream
blanched almonds and angelica to decorate

Mix the butter, 75 g/3 oz of the sugar, one third of the lemon rind and eggs until well mixed. Work in the flour and 75 g/3 oz of the ground almonds and knead to a smooth paste. Wrap and chill for at least 1 hour. Line a flan ring with this almond pastry. Bake blind in a moderate oven (180 C, 350 F, gas 4) for 30 minutes. Cool.

Poach the peaches in the sugar syrup, then remove their skins. Reduce the syrup to a glazing consistency; cool. Beat the cream cheese with the remaining lemon rind, cream, remaining caster sugar and ground almonds. Spread over the pastry base. Arrange the peach halves on top. Brush with syrup glaze and decorate. SERVES 6

Ginger Soufflé

Carol Bowen

4 eggs, separated
75 g/3 oz demerara sugar
½ teaspoon ground ginger
450 ml/¾ pint milk · 1 tablespoon gelatine
6 tablespoons ginger wine
150 ml/¼ pint soured cream
25 g/1 oz preserved ginger, finely chopped
300 ml/½ pint double cream, whipped
crystallised ginger and chopped almonds to
decorate

Prepare a 15-cm/6-in soufflé dish (or six 150-ml/¼-pint soufflé dishes) by tying a double-thick band of grease-proof paper around the dish, extended 5 cm/2 in above the rim. Grease both dish and paper.

Whisk the egg yolks, sugar and ground ginger together in a bowl. Scald the milk in a saucepan and pour on to the egg mixture, whisking constantly. Return to the saucepan and heat, stirring, until the custard thickens and lightly coats the back of the spoon. Do not allow to boil. Dissolve the gelatine in 3 tablespoons of water in a bowl over a saucepan of hot water. Stir into the cooled custard with the ginger wine. Chill until almost set, then stir in the soured cream and preserved ginger. Fold in half the whipped cream. Whisk the egg whites until stiff and fold into the custard. Pour into the dish and chill.

To serve, remove the collar and decorate with the remaining cream, ginger and almonds. SERVES 6

Little Orange Soufflés

Carol Bowen

4 large oranges
4 eggs, separated
50 g/2 oz caster sugar
1 tablespoon Cointreau, Grand Marnier or
frozen concentrated orange juice, thawed
1 tablespoon icing sugar, sifted

Carefully slice the tops from the oranges and scoop out the flesh. Reserve the shells and zig-zag the top edge for decoration, if liked. Remove the rind from the caps of the oranges and cut into very thin julienne strips. Cook the orange strips in a little boiling water for 5 minutes; drain and cool. Extract the juice from the orange flesh and place it in a saucepan. Boil until just 1 tablespoon orange juice remains.

Place the egg yolks and sugar in a bowl and whisk until very thick and creamy. Add the orange rind, warm orange juice and Cointreau, Grand Marnier or concentrated orange juice. In another bowl, whisk the egg whites until they stand in firm peaks. Fold into the orange mixture using a metal spoon. Spoon equal quantities of the soufflé mixture into each orange case. Place on a baking tray and bake in a hot oven (230 c, 450 f, gas 8) for 10 minutes. While the oranges are still in the oven, sprinkle the tops with the icing sugar. Bake for a further 2 to 3 minutes, then serve at once. SERVES 4

Walnut and Strawberry Galette

Carol Bowen

175 g/6 oz butter or margarine
100 g/4 oz caster sugar
grated rind of $\frac{1}{2}$ lemon
175 g/6 oz plain flour
100 g/4 oz walnuts, roughly chopped
FILLING
300 ml/$\frac{1}{2}$ pint whipping cream
1 tablespoon icing sugar
675 g/1$\frac{1}{2}$ lb strawberries, hulled

Grease three baking trays. Cream the butter or margarine and sugar together until light and fluffy. Beat in the lemon rind and fold in the flour. Knead until smooth and chill for 30 minutes.

Divide the dough into three portions and roll each portion out to a 17.5-cm/7-in circle. Pinch the edges of the circles to form a decorative shape. Place on the prepared baking trays and sprinkle the top of each with chopped nuts, pressing them down gently. Bake in a moderate oven (180 c, 350 f, gas 4) for 20 to 25 minutes or until golden. Allow to cool slightly on the trays, then transfer to a wire rack to cool completely.

Whip the cream with the icing sugar until it stands in soft peaks. Slice 450 g/1 lb of the strawberries and fold into two thirds of the cream. Use to sandwich the rounds together. Pipe or spoon the remaining cream in swirls on top of the galette and decorate with the remaining whole strawberries. Chill for 30 minutes before serving.

SERVES 6

Blackcurrant and Ginger Cheesecake

Carol Bowen

100 g/4 oz butter
225 g/8 oz gingernut biscuits, crushed
450 g/1 lb full-fat soft cheese
50 g/2 oz caster sugar
6 tablespoons single cream
575 g/1$\frac{1}{4}$ lb blackcurrants, topped and tailed
15 g/$\frac{1}{2}$ oz gelatine
300 ml/$\frac{1}{2}$ pint double cream
1 egg white, stiffly whisked

Lightly grease a 23-cm/9-in loose-bottomed cake tin with a little of the butter. Melt the remainder in a small saucepan. When melted, add the gingernut crumbs and mix well to coat evenly. Use to line the base of the tin and chill until set.

In a mixing bowl, beat the cream cheese and sugar together until smooth and creamy. Stir in the single cream and 450 g/1 lb of the blackcurrants. Dissolve the gelatine in 2 tablespoons of hot water and stir it into the blackcurrant mixture. Spoon this mixture over the chilled cheesecake crust. Chill until set – about 1 hour.

Meanwhile, whip the double cream until it stands in soft peaks, then fold in the whisked egg white. Using a spoon, swirl this cream mixture over the top of the chilled cheesecake. Use the remaining blackcurrants to sprinkle over the cream and decorate the edge of the cheesecake. Chill for about 15 minutes before serving.

SERVES 6

merican Creamy Cheesecake

— Jane Todd —

oz plus 1 teaspoon butter, melted
/8 oz digestive biscuits, crushed
teaspoon ground cinnamon
450 g/1 lb cream cheese
50 g/2 oz caster sugar
6 tablespoons single cream
15 gelatine, dissolved in 2 tablespoons
hot water
300 ml/½ pint double cream
egg white, stiffly whisked
DECORATION
whipped cream (optional)
fresh fruit (optional)

Lightly g a 23-cm/9-in loose-bottomed cake tin with the teasp f butter.

In a um mixing bowl, combine the crushed biscuits, emaining melted butter and the cinnamon with a wn spoon. Line the base of the tin with this mixture, ing it firmly against the bottom. Set aside.

In ano mixing bowl, beat the cream cheese and sugar tog with a wooden spoon until smooth and creamy. Sn the single cream and gelatine mixture. Whip the ble cream until it stands in soft peaks and fold into theese mixture with the egg white. Spoon the mixt over the biscuit crust. Place in the refrigerato chill for about 1 hour, or until set.

Decorat e cheesecake with whipped cream and fresh fruit, sed, before serving. SERVES 6 TO 8

Chocolate and Orange Mousse

— Jane Todd —

350 g/12 oz plain chocolate
15 g/½ oz unsalted butter
grated rind of 1 orange
1 tablespoon Cointreau
4 eggs, separated
chocolate curls to decorate

Break the chocolate into squares and place them in a basin. Stand the basin over a saucepan of simmering water and leave until the chocolate has melted, stirring occasionally.

Remove the basin from the heat and stir in the butter, orange rind and Cointreau. Mix in the egg yolks. Whisk the whites until stiff, then fold into the chocolate.

Spoon the mousse into individual dishes and chill for at least 1 hour. Decorate with chocolate curls, if used, and serve with crisp dessert biscuits. SERVES 6

Black Forest Gâteau

— Jill Spencer —

3 eggs
125 g/4 oz caster sugar
75 g/3 oz plain flour
15 g/½ oz cocoa
FILLING
1 (425-g/15-oz) can pitted black cherries
1 tablespoon arrowroot
a little kirsch
300 ml/½ pint double cream
grated chocolate to decorate

Place the eggs and sugar in a basin over a saucepan of hot water and whisk until pale and thick. Remove the bowl from the pan and continue to whisk until cool. Sift the flour and cocoa together and gently fold into the mixture, using a metal spoon. Pour into a base-lined and greased 20-cm/8-in cake tin. Bake in a moderately hot oven (190 C, 375 F, gas 5) for 35 to 40 minutes. Turn out and cool on a wire rack.

Drain the juice from the cherries and blend a little into the arrowroot. Bring the remainder of the juice to the boil, then pour on to the blended arrowroot and return to the heat to thicken, stirring continuously. Add the cherries to the syrup and allow to cool.

Cut the cake in half and sprinkle the base with a little kirsch. Whip the cream and place it in a piping bag fitted with a large star nozzle. Pipe a circle of cream round the outside edge of the base. Fill the centre with half the cherry mixture. Sprinkle the second layer of cake with a little kirsch and place on top of the filling. Spread a little cream around the side of the gâteau and press grated chocolate over it. Pipe swirls of cream on top of the gâteau and fill the centre with the remaining cherries. Sprinkle a little grated chocolate on the swirls of cream. SERVES 6 TO 8

Coconut Peach Sundae

—— Carol Bowen ——

600 ml/1 pint double cream
100 g/4 oz desiccated coconut
50 g/2 oz icing sugar, sifted
1 egg, separated
100 g/4 oz plain chocolate, grated
SUNDAE
4 fresh peaches or 8 canned peach halves
1 recipe Melba Sauce (below)
whipped cream and toasted coconut flakes to
decorate

Place the cream and coconut in a saucepan and cook, over a low heat, for about 10 minutes. Stir in the sugar and allow to cool. When cool, beat in the egg yolk and pour into freezer trays. Freeze until half frozen. Whisk the half-frozen ice cream to remove all the ice crystals, then fold in the chocolate. Whisk the egg white until stiff and fold into the ice cream. Freeze until firm.

Meanwhile, if using fresh peaches, poach them in boiling water with a little sugar until they are tender – about 4 minutes. Cool, peel, halve and remove the stones.

To assemble the sundaes, place a scoop of coconut ice cream in the bottom of each of four tall glasses. Top each with two peach halves and melba sauce. Decorate with whipped cream and toasted coconut flakes. Serve with crisp dessert biscuits. SERVES 4

Melba Sauce To prepare a melba sauce, purée 225 g/8 oz raspberries and press the purée through a sieve. Sprinkle in 4 to 5 tablespoons icing sugar, according to taste, and stir until dissolved.

Banana Splits with hot Fudge Sauce

—— Carol Bowen ——

25 g/1 oz plain chocolate
15 g/$\frac{1}{2}$ oz butter
2 tablespoons warm milk
100 g/4 oz soft brown sugar
3 teaspoons golden syrup
2–3 drops vanilla essence
BANANA SPLITS
4 large ripe bananas, peeled
4 portions vanilla ice cream
150 ml/$\frac{1}{4}$ pint double cream
25 g/1 oz walnuts, finely chopped
fresh cherries to decorate (optional)

First prepare the sauce by melting the chocolate in a bowl over a saucepan of simmering water. Add the butter and stir until smooth and glossy. Gradually blend in the milk. Place this mixture with the sugar and golden syrup in a saucepan and heat gently to dissolve the sugar. Bring to the boil and cook for 5 minutes. Add the vanilla essence and keep warm.

Meanwhile, split each banana in half and quickly sandwich together with the ice cream in four individual dishes. Whip the cream until it stands in soft peaks. Spoon or pipe decoratively over the bananas and ice cream. Sprinkle with the nuts and decorate with the cherries, if used. Serve with the hot fudge sauce. SERVES 4

Frozen Christmas Pudding

Carol Bowen

350 g/12 oz mixed dried fruit
100 g/4 oz coloured glacé cherries, chopped
50 g/2 oz chopped mixed peel
50 g/2 oz flaked almonds
3 tablespoons sherry or dark rum
1 tablespoon cocoa, sifted
$\frac{1}{2}$ teaspoon mixed spice
1 egg, separated
50 g/2 oz icing sugar, sifted
300 ml/$\frac{1}{2}$ pint double cream
DECORATION
whipped cream
glacé cherries
angelica

Put the dried fruit, cherries, peel and almonds in a bowl and add the sherry or rum. Leave to soak for 6 hours or overnight.

Add the cocoa to the fruit mixture with the spice and mix well. Add the egg yolk and icing sugar and beat until well combined. Whip the cream until it stands in soft peaks and fold into the fruit mixture. Whisk the egg white until it stands in firm peaks and fold into the cream mixture. Pour into a dampened 1.15-litre/2-pint pudding basin and freeze until firm, about 4 to 6 hours.

When ready to serve, dip the basin briefly into warm water and invert it on to a serving dish. Leave for about 1 hour in the refrigerator so that the pudding softens a little. Decorate with whipped cream, glacé cherries and angelica. Top with a sprig of holly and cut into wedges to serve. SERVES 6 TO 8

Brown Bread Ice Cream

Carol Bowen

300 ml/$\frac{1}{2}$ pint double cream
150 ml/$\frac{1}{4}$ pint single cream
75 g/3 oz icing sugar, sifted
100 g/4 oz fresh brown breadcrumbs
1 tablespoon dark rum (optional)
2 eggs, separated
sliced strawberries to decorate (optional)

This traditional English ice cream recipe is far more delicious than it sounds.

Whip the double cream until just stiff, then gradually whisk in the single cream. Fold in the icing sugar and breadcrumbs. Lightly beat the rum, if used, with the egg yolks and stir into the cream mixture.

Whisk the egg whites until they stand in stiff peaks and fold into the cream mixture. Pour the mixture into freezer trays or into a 1.15-litre/2-pint decorative ice cream mould and freeze for about 3 to 4 hours or until firm. Turn out and serve with sliced strawberries and crisp dessert biscuits. SERVES 4 TO 6

Baking

Home-baked breads and cakes are always far superior to those you can buy, so why not treat the family to a hot fresh loaf, a special fruit cake or some crunchy biscuits? All these basic recipes are here, and many more too.

Battenburg, Swiss Roll, Lattice Tart and Bread Rolls

Bread Rolls

(ILLUSTRATED ON PREVIOUS PAGE)

Make up a single quantity of the bread dough according to the instructions for white bread. When the dough has risen once, instead of dividing it between two loaf tins as instructed, cut it into about 18 or 20 equal portions. Shape each portion into a roll, making some into tiny cottage loaves, twists and plaits or knots, as illustrated. Place the shaped rolls on greased baking trays, cover with oiled cling film and leave to rise in a warm place until doubled in size.

Glaze the rolls with a little beaten egg and water and sprinkle poppy seeds, sesame seeds or chopped nuts over the top. Bake in a hot oven (230 C, 450 F, gas 8) for 15 to 20 minutes. Cool the rolls on a wire rack. MAKES 18 TO 20

Lattice Tart

Bridget Jones

(ILLUSTRATED ON PREVIOUS PAGE)

450 g/1 lb shortcrust pastry (page 87)
350 g/12 oz jam

Roll out half the pastry and use to line a 15-cm/8-in loose-bottomed flan tin. Prick the base all over with a fork and spread the jam over the flan.

Roll out the remaining pastry to form an oblong measuring 15 cm/8 in down one side. Cut this piece of pastry into strips measuring about 1 cm/$\frac{1}{2}$ in wide and lay these across the jam in a lattice pattern.

Bake in a moderately hot oven (200 C, 400 F, gas 6) for about 40 minutes, or until golden brown and cooked. Serve hot or cold. SERVES 6

Farmhouse Loaf

Jill Spencer

100 g/4 oz self-raising flour
100 g/4 oz wholemeal flour
pinch of grated nutmeg
$\frac{1}{2}$ teaspoon bicarbonate of soda
75 g/3 oz butter or margarine
100 g/4 oz caster sugar
50 g/2 oz raisins
25 g/1 oz glacé cherries
25 g/1 oz sultanas
25 g/1 oz chopped mixed peel
grated rind of 1 lemon
1 egg, beaten
6 tablespoons milk

Place the flours, nutmeg and bicarbonate of soda in a mixing bowl and rub in the butter until the mixture resembles fine breadcrumbs. Add the sugar, fruits, peel and lemon rind, then mix in the egg and milk to give a soft, dropping consistency. Place in a lined and greased 450-g/1-lb loaf tin. Bake in a moderate oven (180 C, 350 F, gas 4) for 50 to 60 minutes. Turn out and cool on a wire rack. Serve sliced and spread with butter. MAKES ONE 450-G / 1-LB LOAF

White Bread

Mary Berry

15 g/½ oz lard
675 g/1½ lb plain flour
1 tablespoon salt
YEAST LIQUID
1 teaspoon sugar
450 ml/¾ pint warm water
2 teaspoons dried yeast

First prepare the yeast liquid: dissolve the sugar in the water and sprinkle the yeast on top, then leave until frothy – about 10 minutes.

Rub the lard into the flour and salt and mix in the yeast liquid. Work to a firm dough, until the sides of the bowl are clean. Turn on to a lightly floured surface and knead thoroughly for about 10 minutes.

Place the dough in a lightly greased polythene bag, tie the bag loosely and leave to rise until double in size. Remove the polythene and turn the dough out on to a lightly floured surface. Knead lightly. Grease two 450-g/1-lb loaf tins. Divide the dough in half, stretch each piece into an oblong the same width as the tins and fold over in three. With the seam underneath, smooth over the top and place the loaf in the tin, tucking in the folded ends so that they face the base of the tin. Place the tins inside greased polythene bags and leave the dough to rise until it comes to the top of the tins.

Bake the bread loaves in a hot oven (230 C, 450 F, gas 8) for 30 to 40 minutes. Turn them out of the tins and leave to cool on a wire rack. MAKES TWO 450-G/1-LB LOAVES

Cheese and Celery Loaf

Mary Berry

450 g/1 lb self-raising flour
2 teaspoons salt
40 g/1½ oz butter
3 large sticks celery, chopped
1 clove garlic, crushed
175 g/6 oz mature Cheddar cheese, grated
1 egg
scant 300 ml/½ pint milk

Grease a 1-kg/2-lb loaf tin. Sift the flour and salt into a bowl and rub in the fat until the mixture resembles fine breadcrumbs.

Add the celery, garlic and cheese to the flour mixture. Beat the egg and milk together, add gradually to the dry ingredients and mix to form a soft dough. Knead the dough lightly and quickly on a floured surface, then shape it into an oblong. Place in the loaf tin and bake in a hot oven (220 C, 425 F, gas 7) for about 55 minutes.

Turn out and cool on a wire rack. Serve freshly cooked, with butter. MAKES ONE 1-KG/2-LB LOAF

Quick Wholemeal Bread

———— Janet Hunt ————

1.4 kg/3 lb plain wholemeal flour
generous pinch of salt
25 g/1 oz fresh yeast
1 litre/1¾ pints lukewarm water
1 teaspoon raw brown sugar, honey or
molasses

Mix the flour and salt together in a warmed bowl. Cream the yeast with about one third of the water, the sugar, honey or molasses, then set it aside in a warm place for 5 minutes, until frothy.

Make a well in the centre of the flour and pour in the yeast liquid, followed by the rest of the water. Mix the flour into the liquid with a wooden spoon, adding a little more warm water if it seems too dry. Stir thoroughly for several minutes; use your hands if you find it easier. Set the oven at hot (230 C, 450 F, gas 8). Thoroughly grease two 1-kg/2-lb loaf tins and turn the dough into them. Leave the tins in a warm, draught-free spot until the dough has risen to the top of each tin (this can take anything up to 1 hour). Bake the bread for 5 minutes, then lower the heat to moderately hot (200 C, 400 F, gas 6) and continue to bake for 30 minutes more. Turn the bread out of the tins and test to see if it is done by tapping the base of each loaf with your knuckles – if it sounds hollow, put it on a wire rack to cool; if not, do not replace it in its tin, but return it to the oven, stand it upside down and bake the loaf for a further 5 minutes. MAKES TWO 1-KG/2-LB LOAVES

Soda Bread

———— Janet Hunt ————

450 g/1 lb wholemeal flour
1 teaspoon bicarbonate of soda
1 teaspoon cream of tartar
pinch of salt
about 300 ml/½ pint milk and warm water

Set the oven at moderately hot (190 C, 375 F, gas 5). Mix the flour, soda, cream of tartar and salt. Stir in enough liquid to give a moist dough – you may need to adjust the quantity to get the right consistency.

Turn the dough on to a floured board, dust it with flour and, using your hands, pat it into one large or two small rounds – the traditional shape for soda bread. Put the bread on a lightly greased baking sheet, flatten it slightly and cut a large cross in the top of each loaf. Bake for 40 minutes or until the bread is firm to the touch and sounds hollow when tapped. Cool on a wire rack. Eat while fresh as this bread does not keep very well. MAKES ONE LARGE OR TWO SMALL LOAVES

Onion and Herb Loaf

———— Carol Bowen ————

15 g/½ oz fresh yeast
½ teaspoon sugar
6 tablespoons lukewarm water
6 tablespoons milk
1 tablespoon butter or margarine
275 g/10 oz wholemeal flour
1 teaspoon salt
1 teaspoon finely chopped sage
2 teaspoons finely chopped savory
1 small onion, peeled and minced

Cream the yeast with the sugar and 2 tablespoons of the water to form a smooth paste. Set aside in a warm place for about 15 to 20 minutes, or until the yeast mixture has risen and is frothy.

Bring the milk to just under boiling point, remove from the heat, then add the butter or margarine and the remaining water. Set aside and leave until lukewarm.

Put the flour and salt into a warmed bowl. Sprinkle with the herbs and onion. Make a well in the centre of the flour and pour in the yeast and milk mixtures. Draw the flour into the liquid and mix until the dough comes away from the sides of the bowl.

Turn out on to a lightly floured surface and knead for 10 minutes. Form the dough into a ball and return it to the clean bowl. Cover with a damp cloth or cling film and leave to prove in a warm place for 1 to 1½ hours, or until the dough has doubled in bulk.

Lightly grease a 450-g/1-lb loaf tin and set aside. Turn the dough out on to a lightly floured surface and knead for 8 to 10 minutes. Form the dough into a loaf and place it in the tin. Cover with a damp cloth or cling film and leave to prove for 30 to 45 minutes, or until the dough has doubled in bulk again. Bake in a moderately hot oven (200 C, 400 F, gas 6) for 1 hour. Cool on a wire rack. MAKES ONE 450-G/1-LB LOAF

Chopped Peanut Loaf

Audrey Ellis

100 g/4 oz wholemeal flour
100 g/4 oz plain flour
2 teaspoons baking powder
$\frac{1}{4}$ teaspoon salt
100 g/4 oz peanut butter
1 egg
3 tablespoons clear honey
250 ml/8 fl oz milk
25 g/1 oz margarine, melted
1 teaspoon grated lemon rind
50 g/2 oz salted peanuts, chopped

Mix the flours, baking powder and salt in a large bowl. Rub in the peanut butter until the mixture is crumbly. Lightly beat the egg and add to the flour mixture with the honey, milk, melted margarine and lemon rind. Stir until just combined, then fold in the chopped peanuts.

Spoon the mixture into a 1-kg/2-lb loaf tin and bake in a moderate oven (180 C, 350 F, gas 4) for 1 hour. Cool for 10 minutes in the tin, then turn out on to a wire rack. MAKES ONE 1-KG/2-LB LOAF

Welsh Currant Bread

Mary Berry

75 g/3 oz margarine
350 g/12 oz plain flour
75 g/3 oz demerara sugar
1 teaspoon salt
1 teaspoon mixed spice
675 g/1$\frac{1}{2}$ lb mixed seedless raisins, currants, sultanas and candied peel
1 egg, beaten
YEAST LIQUID
100 g/4 oz plain flour
1$\frac{1}{2}$ teaspoons dried yeast
1 teaspoon sugar
300 ml/$\frac{1}{2}$ pint warm water less 6 tablespoons
honey for glazing

Put the flour for the yeast liquid into a large bowl and make a well in the middle. Mix the yeast, sugar and water in the well in the flour. Set aside until frothy – about 20 minutes.

Rub the margarine into the 350 g/12 oz flour, then mix in the sugar, salt, spice and fruit. Add the egg and the flour mixture to the yeast liquid. Mix well. Knead the dough thoroughly on a lightly floured surface. Place in a greased polythene bag, loosely tied, and allow to rise until double in size.

Lightly knead the dough to knock out the air bubbles. Divide in half and shape to fit two greased 450-g/1-lb loaf tins. Place each tin in a greased polythene bag and allow the dough to rise to 2.5 cm/1 in above the top of the tins. Bake in a moderate oven (180 C, 350 F, gas 4) for 50 to 60 minutes. Turn out on to a wire rack and glaze with honey while still hot. MAKES TWO 450-G/1-LB LOAVES

Battenburg

Jill Spencer

175 g/6 oz butter or margarine
175 g/6 oz caster sugar
3 eggs
175 g/6 oz self-raising flour
1 tablespoon cocoa
1 tablespoon hot water
grated rind of 1 lemon
lemon curd
450 g/1 lb almond paste
caster sugar

Mix the cake as for the Basic Victoria Sandwich (above). Divide the mixture in half. To one half add the cocoa blended in hot water, and to the other add the lemon rind. Line and grease an 18-cm/7-in square cake tin and divide down the middle with a strip of folded greaseproof paper. Place the chocolate mixture in one side and the lemon in the other. Bake in a moderate oven (160 C, 325 F, gas 3) for 40 to 50 minutes.

Trim the edges of the cooled cake and cut each half in two lengthways, making four strips. Join alternate colours together in two layers, sandwiching them with lemon curd.

Roll the almond paste into an oblong 20 × 37-cm/ 8 × 15-in. Spread the outside of the assembled cake with lemon curd and place it in the middle of the almond paste. Carefully ease the almond paste around the cake with the join underneath. Trim and finish as shown in the picture.

Meringues

Jill Spencer

2 egg whites
100 g/4 oz caster sugar
FILLING AND DECORATION
300 ml/½ pint double cream
a few glacé cherries
angelica leaves

Whisk the egg whites until stiff. Gradually whisk in half the sugar then carefully fold in the remainder using a metal spoon. Transfer the mixture to a piping bag fitted with a large star nozzle and pipe small meringues on to greased baking trays. Dry out in a very cool oven (110 C, 225 F, gas ¼) for 3½ to 4 hours. Cool on a wire rack.

Whip the cream until stiff and use to sandwich the meringues together, then decorate with pieces of cherry and angelica leaves. MAKES ABOUT 12

Basic Victoria Sandwich

Jill Spencer

100 g/4 oz butter or margarine
100 g/4 oz caster sugar
2 eggs
100 g/4 oz self-raising flour
3–4 tablespoons raspberry jam
icing sugar

Cream the butter and sugar together until light and fluffy. Beat in the eggs one at a time, adding a little of the flour with the second egg. Fold in the remaining flour using a metal spoon. Place the mixture in a base-lined and greased 20-cm/8-in sandwich tin or two 18-cm/7-in sandwich tins. Bake in a moderate oven (160 C, 325 F, gas 3), 35 to 40 minutes for the 20-cm/8-in cake, and 25 to 35 minutes for the 18-cm/7-in cakes. Turn out and cool on a wire rack.

Split the larger cake and sandwich the cakes or two halves with the raspberry jam. Lay a doily on top of the cake and dust with icing sugar. Carefully lift off the doily to leave a design on the surface of the cake.

Swiss Roll

Mary Berry

3 large eggs, at room temperature
3 oz caster sugar, warmed
3 oz self-raising flour, sifted
caster sugar for dredging
4 tablespoons raspberry jam, warmed

Line and grease a 23 × 30-cm/9 × 12-in Swiss roll tin. Whisk the eggs with the sugar until light and creamy and the whisk leaves a trail when lifted out of the mixture. Fold in the flour, using a metal spoon.

Turn into the prepared tin and smooth the mixture level with a palette knife. Bake in a hot oven (220 c, 425 f, gas 7) for 7 to 10 minutes, until the sponge begins to shrink from the edges of the tin and is pale golden.

Turn out on to a sheet of greaseproof paper dredged with caster sugar. Trim the edges of the sponge, spread it with warmed jam and roll up tightly. Dredge with caster sugar and cool on a wire rack.

Cherry Cake

Mary Berry

225 g/8 oz glacé cherries
75 g/3 oz self-raising flour
75 g/3 oz plain flour
pinch of salt
175 g/6 oz butter
175 g/6 oz caster sugar
finely grated rind of 1 lemon
3 eggs, beaten
75 g/3 oz ground almonds
a little milk (if necessary)

Grease an 18-cm/7-in round cake tin and line it with greased greaseproof paper. Rinse, dry and halve the cherries. Sift the flours and salt together twice, then toss the cherries into a little of the flour. Cream the butter, sugar and lemon rind together until the mixture is pale and creamy. Add the beaten eggs a little at a time, beating well after each addition and keeping the mixture stiff. Add a tablespoon of the flour with the last amount of egg. Fold in the flour, cherries and ground almonds, adding a little milk to make a fairly stiff dropping consistency; the stiff consistency will help to keep the cherries suspended evenly in the cake.

Turn the mixture into the prepared tin and bake in a moderate oven (180 c, 350 f, gas 4) for about 1 hour 20 minutes, or until a skewer inserted in the centre of the cake comes out clean.

Leave the cake to cool in the tin for 5 minutes, then turn it out on to a wire rack to finish cooling. When cold remove the cooking paper and wrap the cake in foil or store it in an airtight tin.

Traditional Christmas Cake

Mary Berry

250 g/9 oz plain flour
¼ teaspoon salt
1 teaspoon mixed spice
225 g/8 oz butter
225 g/8 oz soft brown sugar
4 eggs, lightly beaten
1–2 tablespoons black treacle
350 g/12 oz seedless raisins
350 g/12 oz sultanas · 350 g/12 oz currants
50 g/2 oz candied peel, chopped
75 g/3 oz glacé cherries, quartered
50 g/2 oz blanched almonds, chopped
2 tablespoons brandy

Line the base and side of a 20-cm/8-in round cake tin with a double layer of greaseproof paper, then tie a double band of brown paper, 2.5 cm/1 in wider than the depth of the tin, round the outside.

Sift the flour, salt and spice into a large bowl. Cream the butter and sugar together and gradually beat in the eggs. Stir in the treacle, then the flour, dried fruit, peel, cherries and almonds. Turn the mixture into the prepared tin and bake in a cool oven (150 c, 300 f, gas 2) for 3 hours, then reduce the oven to (140 c, 275 f, gas 1) and bake for a further 1 to 1½ hours, or until a skewer inserted into the cake comes out clean.

Cool the cake in the tin for 10 minutes, then on a wire rack. Remove the paper. Turn the cake upside down, pierce it with a skewer and spoon over the brandy. Store, when cold, wrapped in greaseproof paper and foil, in an airtight tin.

Christmas Cake Icing

Mary Berry

ALMOND PASTE
350 g/12 oz ground almonds
75 g/6 oz caster sugar
75 g/6 oz icing sugar, sifted
3 egg whites
a few drops of almond essence
3 tablespoons apricot jam, sieved
ROYAL ICING
4 egg whites
1 kg/2 lb icing sugar, sifted
4 teaspoons lemon juice
2 teaspoons glycerine

Mix the almonds and sugars in a bowl, then blend in the egg whites and almond essence to make a soft paste. Knead until smooth and divide into three equal portions. Roll one piece out on a sugared board to a 20-cm/8-in circle. Roll the remaining two thirds to a strip the same depth as the cake, and long enough to go all the way round the edge. Brush the side of the cake with apricot jam. Place the long strip round the side and press firmly to join. Place the circle of paste on top of the cake. Allow to dry for at least 3 days before icing.

To make the royal icing, whisk the egg whites until they become frothy. Add the sugar, a tablespoon at a time, and beat well after each addition. Finally beat in the lemon juice and glycerine. To prevent the icing from hardening, cover the bowl with a damp cloth.

Spread the icing thickly over the top and round the side of the cake, then draw it up in peaks with the handle of a teaspoon. Leave to set for a day, then arrange any decorations on top.

Coffee Ginger Cake

— *Mary Berry* —

4 eggs
75 g/3 oz caster sugar
75 g/3 oz plain flour, sifted
FILLING
350 g/12 oz icing sugar, sifted
1 tablespoon coffee essence
2 tablespoons rum · 175 g/6 oz butter
50 g/2 oz crystallised ginger, chopped
ICING
175 g/6 oz icing sugar, sifted
1 tablespoon coffee essence
50 g/2 oz blanched almonds, chopped

Grease two 19-cm/7½-in straight-sided sandwich tins and line the bases with circles of greased greaseproof paper. Put the eggs and sugar in a bowl placed over a pan of hot water. Whisk until the mixture is pale and thick. Remove from the heat and carefully fold in the flour. Divide the mixture between the tins and bake in a moderately hot oven (190 C, 375 F, gas 5) for 20 to 25 minutes or until each sponge springs back when lightly pressed. Cool on a wire rack. Slice each cake horizontally in half.

Blend together the icing sugar, coffee essence and rum. Cream the butter until it is soft, then gradually add the icing sugar mixture and beat well. Mix the chopped ginger with three quarters of the filling and use to sandwich the four cakes together. Spread more filling thinly over the side of the cake.

Make a fairly thick glacé icing with the icing sugar, coffee essence and a little water. Use to cover the top of the cake. Lightly toast the almonds and press them against the sides of the cake. Use any remaining filling to pipe rosettes round the top edge of the cake.

Tipsy Ring

— *Jill Spencer* —

100 g/4 oz butter or margarine
100 g/4 oz caster sugar
5 tablespoons ginger wine
2 eggs
100 g/4 oz self-raising flour
25 g/1 oz cocoa
ICING AND DECORATION
175 g/6 oz plain chocolate
50 g/2 oz butter
150 ml/¼ pint double cream
a few pieces of crystallised ginger

Cream the butter with the sugar and 2 tablespoons of the ginger wine until pale and fluffy. Gradually beat in the eggs. Sift the flour with the cocoa and fold into the creamed mixture using a metal spoon. Turn into a well greased 23-cm/9-in ring tin and bake in a moderate oven (160 C, 325 F, gas 3) for 40 to 45 minutes. Turn out and cool on a wire rack. While the cake is still warm, drizzle the remaining ginger wine over it, until absorbed.

Melt the chocolate with the butter for the icing. Allow to cool slightly, then drizzle the icing over the cake. Whip the cream until stiff and, using a piping bag fitted with a large star nozzle, pipe the cream along the top of the cake. Decorate with pieces of crystallised ginger.

Honey Squares

Jill Spencer

175 g/6 oz thick honey
175 g/6 oz butter or margarine
75 g/3 oz demerara sugar
100 g/4 oz sultanas
75 g/3 oz blanched almonds, chopped
grated rind of 2 oranges
juice of $\frac{1}{2}$ orange
2 eggs, lightly beaten
200 g/7 oz self-raising flour
1 teaspoon baking powder
$\frac{1}{2}$ teaspoon ground cinnamon
TOPPING
100 g/4 oz blanched almonds
5 tablespoons thick honey
50 g/2 oz sultanas
generous pinch of cinnamon
grated rind of 1 orange

Melt the honey, butter or margarine and sugar together with the sultanas, almonds, orange rind and juice over a gentle heat; cool slightly. Beat in the eggs. Sift the dry ingredients and beat in to give a smooth batter.

Pour into a lined and greased 18×26-cm/$7 \times 10\frac{1}{2}$-in shallow tin and bake in a moderate oven (160 C, 325 F, gas 3) for 40 to 50 minutes. Cool slightly in the tin, then mix all the ingredients for the topping. Warm slightly if necessary, spread on top of the cake and leave to cool. Cut the cake into squares. MAKES 12

Lemon Honey Buns

Jill Spencer

100 g/4 oz butter or margarine
50 g/2 oz soft brown sugar
100 g/4 oz thick honey
grated rind and juice of 1 lemon
2 eggs, lightly beaten
225 g/8 oz self-raising flour
1 teaspoon baking powder
ICING
225 g/8 oz icing sugar, sifted
2–3 tablespoons lemon juice
pared lemon rind to decorate

Melt the butter or margarine, sugar and honey together with the lemon rind and juice over a gentle heat, stirring occasionally. Leave to cool slightly, then beat in the eggs. Sift the flour and baking powder together and beat into the melted mixture to give a smooth, thick batter.

Divide between greased, deep patty tins and bake in a moderately hot oven (190 C, 375 F, gas 5) for 15 to 20 minutes. Cool on a wire rack. Beat the icing sugar and lemon juice together until smooth, then pour it over the cakes and top with lemon rind. MAKES 12 TO 14

Almond Macaroons

Jill Spencer

2 egg whites
100 g/4 oz caster sugar
100 g/4 oz ground almonds
1 teaspoon ground rice
few drops of almond essence
halved almonds

Whisk the egg whites until stiff. Gradually whisk in the sugar and continue whisking until the mixture is thick and glossy. Stir in the ground almonds, ground rice and a few drops of almond essence.

Place the mixture in a piping bag fitted with a large plain nozzle. Place sheets of rice paper on baking trays and pipe small circles of the mixture on to the paper. Place an almond on top of each macaroon and bake in a moderate oven (160 c, 325 f, gas 3) for 15 to 20 minutes. Carefully remove as much of the rice paper as possible from around the macaroons and cool them on a wire rack. MAKES ABOUT 20

Peanut Cookies

Jill Spencer

50 g/2 oz butter or margarine, softened
50 g/2 oz soft brown sugar
50 g/2 oz salted peanuts, roughly chopped
grated rind of 1 orange
75 g/3 oz self-raising flour
1 tablespoon orange juice

Cream the butter or margarine and sugar until light and fluffy, then mix in all the remaining ingredients to form a soft dough. Take small pieces of dough, about the size of a walnut, and roll them into balls. Place well apart on greased baking trays, flatten with a fork and bake in a moderate oven (180 c, 350 f, gas 4) for 10 to 12 minutes. Remove and cool on a wire rack. MAKES ABOUT 12

Orange Shortbread

Mary Berry

100 g/4 oz plain flour
50 g/2 oz cornflour
100 g/4 oz butter
50 g/2 oz caster sugar
grated rind of 1 orange
caster sugar to sprinkle

Sift the flour and cornflour together. Cream the butter until soft, then add the caster sugar and beat until the mixture is pale and creamy. Gradually work the orange rind and flours into the mixture.

Lift the shortbread on to a large baking tray. Roll it out to give a 20-cm/8-in circle. Pinch the edges and prick the shortbread with a fork. Cut into sections with the blunt edge of a knife, then sprinkle with a little caster sugar.

Chill for 15 minutes, then bake in a moderate oven (160 C, 325 F, gas 3) for 35 minutes or until pale golden. Cool on the baking tray for a few minutes, then transfer to a wire rack to cool. MAKES 12

Flapjacks

Mary Berry

100 g/4 oz margarine
4 tablespoons golden syrup
75 g/3 oz sugar
225 g/8 oz rolled oats
$\frac{1}{4}$ teaspoon salt

Grease a 19-cm/7$\frac{1}{2}$-in square, shallow tin. Put the margarine and syrup in a pan over a low heat until the margarine has melted. Remove from the heat and add the sugar, oats and salt. Mix thoroughly.

Turn the mixture into the prepared tin and cook in a moderate oven (160 C, 325 F, gas 3) for 30 to 40 minutes, until golden brown.

Leave to cool in the tin for 5 minutes. Cut the flapjacks into bars and cool completely on a wire rack. MAKES 12

Preserving

There is nothing more satisfying than the sight of a shelf
stocked with freshly potted preserves. Jams and jellies,
chutneys and pickles are all included in this chapter, ready
for the day when you have both the time and inclination
as well as the ingredients to make them.

Making Jams and Jellies

For a successful preserve, it is important to use good quality fruit. Select fruit which is not quite ripe as it contains the most pectin – the substance which is essential for making the jam set. Follow the chart on the opposite page for the quantities of water and sugar and refer to the pectin/acid column to check whether there is any need to add lemon juice or apple pulp. Wrap all the trimmings (peel, pips, cores and stones) securely in muslin and cook them with the fruit, then thoroughly squeeze out the package to extract all the pectin.

Prepare the fruit according to its type, slicing or halving the pieces, then cook it in a large pan with the liquid, or just a little of the sugar to bring out the juice, until the fruit is soft. Add the bulk of sugar when the fruit is cooked, preferably warming the sugar first so the temperature of the mixture is not drastically reduced. Cook slowly, stirring continuously, until the sugar has dissolved completely, then bring to a rolling boil and boil hard until setting point is reached.

There are three ways of testing for setting – the thermometer test, the saucer test and the flake test. Using a sugar thermometer is the most accurate method. The thermometer should be placed well into the jam, but it should not touch the base of the saucepan. Most jams and jellies set at 104c/220f. The next most reliable is the saucer test: drop a little of the hot preserve on to a cool saucer and leave it to set for a few minutes. If setting point is reached, the surface should wrinkle when pushed with the finger. The flake test is the least accurate – drop a little of the preserve off the edge of a wooden spoon; as it drops it should form flakes.

Pour the preserve into thoroughly cleaned, heated jars (you can heat the jars by filling them with boiling water or by standing them in a warm oven), cover the surfaces with waxed discs, waxed sides down, and top with airtight lids or cellophane. Store the preserve in a cool, dry place.

Apple Pulp Rinse and roughly chop 450 g/1 lb cooking apples. Place them in a saucepan with 300 ml/$\frac{1}{2}$ pint water, bring to the boil and cook, covered, for about 20 to 25 minutes or until the fruit is reduced to a pulp. Press this pulp through a sieve and use the purée for adding pectin to jams prepared from fruits which have a low pectin content. This quantity is sufficient to set 1.5 kg/3 lb fruit.

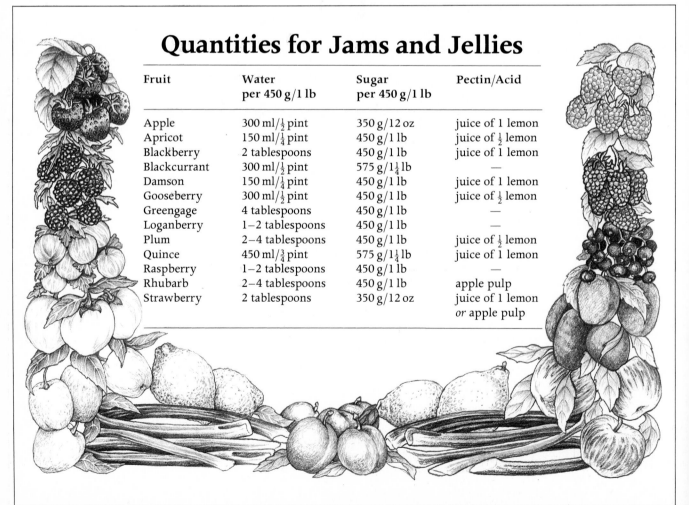

Quantities for Jams and Jellies

Fruit	Water per 450 g/1 lb	Sugar per 450 g/1 lb	Pectin/Acid
Apple	300 ml/$\frac{1}{2}$ pint	350 g/12 oz	juice of 1 lemon
Apricot	150 ml/$\frac{1}{4}$ pint	450 g/1 lb	juice of $\frac{1}{2}$ lemon
Blackberry	2 tablespoons	450 g/1 lb	juice of 1 lemon
Blackcurrant	300 ml/$\frac{1}{2}$ pint	575 g/1$\frac{1}{4}$ lb	—
Damson	150 ml/$\frac{1}{4}$ pint	450 g/1 lb	juice of 1 lemon
Gooseberry	300 ml/$\frac{1}{2}$ pint	450 g/1 lb	juice of $\frac{1}{2}$ lemon
Greengage	4 tablespoons	450 g/1 lb	—
Loganberry	1–2 tablespoons	450 g/1 lb	—
Plum	2–4 tablespoons	450 g/1 lb	juice of $\frac{1}{2}$ lemon
Quince	450 ml/$\frac{3}{4}$ pint	575 g/1$\frac{1}{4}$ lb	juice of 1 lemon
Raspberry	1–2 tablespoons	450 g/1 lb	—
Rhubarb	2–4 tablespoons	450 g/1 lb	apple pulp
Strawberry	2 tablespoons	350 g/12 oz	juice of 1 lemon *or* apple pulp

Ginger Marmalade

—— Bridget Jones ——

8 lemons
2 large oranges
2.25 litres/4 pints water
100 g/4 oz fresh root ginger
1.5 kg/3 lb sugar

Pare the rind from the lemons and oranges and cut it into thin strips. Squeeze the juice from the fruit and mix it in a large saucepan with the rinds and water. Thinly peel the ginger, slice and finely shred it, then add it to the pan.

Chop the remainder of the lemons and oranges, including the pith, and tie them up in a piece of clean muslin. Add the muslin bag to the pan and bring the mixture to the boil. Reduce the heat, cover the pan and simmer for 2 hours or until the ginger and fruit rinds are completely tender. Take the pan off the heat and leave it to stand until the muslin is cool enough to handle, then squeeze all the juices out of it into the marmalade.

Pour the sugar into the pan and stir the mixture over a gentle heat until the sugar has completely dissolved. Bring to the boil and boil hard to setting point. Use a slotted spoon to remove the scum from the top of the marmalade, then allow it to stand for about 15 to 20 minutes. Stir it thoroughly before pouring it into warmed pots. Cover with waxed discs, waxed sides down and allow to cool before topping the pots with lids or cellophane covers. MAKES ABOUT 2.25 KG / 5 LB

Apricot and Loganberry Jam

Bridget Jones

1 kg/2 lb fresh apricots
300 ml/½ pint water
450 g/1 lb loganberries
1.5 kg/3 lb sugar
25 g/1 oz butter

Halve and stone the apricots. Crack the stones and remove the kernels. Mix the fruit with their kernels in a large saucepan and pour in the water. Bring to the boil and reduce the heat, then cook the apricots, uncovered, for 5 to 10 minutes until they are just soft.

Add the loganberries to the pan and gradually stir in the sugar. Stir the mixture over a gentle heat until the sugar has dissolved completely, bring it to the boil and boil hard until setting point is reached.

Stir in the butter to disperse the scum and transfer the jam to warmed pots. Cover with waxed discs, waxed sides down, and leave to cool completely. Top the pots with pieces of cellophane or airtight lids and label them neatly. MAKES ABOUT 2.25 KG/5 LB

Apple and Mandarin Jam

Bridget Jones

450 g/1 lb mandarins
450 g/1 lb cooking apples
600 ml/1 pint water
juice of 2 lemons
800 g/1¾ lb sugar

Halve the mandarins and carefully remove all the pips. Chop the flesh and peel quite finely, removing any further pips. Peel, core and slice the apples. Mix the apple peelings and core with pips from the mandarins and tie them securely in a piece of clean muslin.

Put all the chopped fruit in a large saucepan and pour in the water. Add the muslin package and bring to the boil. Cover the pan, reduce the heat and simmer the mixture gently for 1 hour or until the fruit is soft.

Allow to cool until the muslin can be handled, then squeeze all the juices out of it into the jam. Pour in the lemon juice and sugar and heat the jam gently, stirring continuously, until the sugar has completely dissolved. Bring it to the boil and boil hard to setting point.

Pour the jam into warmed pots and top each with a waxed disc, waxed side down. Allow to cool before covering the pots with lids or pieces of cellophane. MAKES ABOUT 1 KG/2 LB

Cherry and Apple Jam

Bridget Jones

1 kg/2 lb cherries
1 kg/2 lb cooking apples
juice of 2 lemons
1.15 litres/2 pints water
1.25 g/2½ lb sugar
15 g/½ oz butter

Stone the cherries and place the stones in a large saucepan. Peel, core and thickly slice the cooking apples, then sprinkle the slices with the lemon juice and set them aside. Add the apple trimmings to the pan with the cherry stones and pour in the water. Bring to the boil and cook, uncovered, until the liquid is reduced to about one third of its original quantity. This will take about 1 hour.

Press the resulting pulp through a fine sieve and return it to the rinsed-out saucepan. Add the prepared cherries and apples and bring the mixture to the boil. Cover the pan and simmer gently, stirring occasionally, for 10 to 15 minutes, until the fruit is soft.

Pour in the sugar and heat gently, stirring, until the sugar has dissolved. Bring the jam to a rapid boil and boil hard to setting point. Stir in the butter to disperse any scum and pot the jam into warmed jars. Cover the surfaces with waxed paper discs, waxed sides down, and allow to cool. Top the pots with cellophane covers or lids and label them when cold. MAKES ABOUT 2.25 KG/5 LB

Blackcurrant Butter

Bridget Jones

450 g/1 lb cooking apples
1 kg/2 lb blackcurrants
600 ml/1 pint water
sugar
juice of 2 large lemons

Rinse and roughly chop the apples and place them in a large saucepan with the blackcurrants and water. Bring to the boil, cover the pan and reduce the heat. Simmer the fruit for 2 hours.

Allow it to cool slightly, then press it through a fine sieve and weigh the resulting pulp. For each 450 g/1 lb pulp allow 350 g/12 oz sugar. Return the pulp to the pan with the sugar and lemon juice and stir the mixture over a gentle heat until the sugar has dissolved. Bring it to the boil and boil for 30 to 40 minutes, stirring frequently, until the butter has thickened to a creamy consistency and a spoon dipped into it will leave a ribbon trail on the surface.

Transfer the butter to warmed pots and top each with a disc of waxed paper, waxed side down. Leave it to cool and cover the pots with pieces of cellophane or airtight lids. MAKES ABOUT 1 KG/2 LB

Apricot and Date Jam

Bridget Jones

1 kg/2 lb fresh apricots
225 g/8 oz fresh dates
600 ml/1 pint water
grated rind of 1 orange
1.25 kg/2½ lb sugar
25 g/1 oz butter

Halve and stone the apricots. Crack the stones and take out the kernels. Place the fruit and their kernels in a large saucepan. Halve and stone the dates, removing and discarding their skins, and place them in the saucepan. Pour in the water, add the orange rind and bring to the boil. Reduce the heat and simmer the fruit, uncovered, for 30 minutes.

Add the sugar to the jam and stir it over a low heat until the sugar has completely dissolved. Bring to the boil and boil rapidly until setting point is reached. Add the butter to the pan, stirring it in to disperse the scum.

Pot the jam in warmed pots and cover the surface of each with a disc of waxed paper, waxed side down. Leave to cool, then cover the pots and label them. MAKES ABOUT 1.5 KG/3 LB

Lemon Curd

Bridget Jones

(ILLUSTRATED ON PREVIOUS PAGE)

grated rind and juice of 3 large lemons
100 g/4 oz butter, cut into pieces
3 large eggs, beaten
350 g/12 oz caster sugar

Mix all the ingredients in the top of a double saucepan or in a large basin held over a pan of gently simmering water. Do not allow the water to boil or the curd may overheat and curdle.

Stir the mixture until the sugar has dissolved, then continue cooking, stirring frequently, until the eggs are cooked and the mixture has thickened enough to coat the back of a wooden spoon.

Pour the curd into clean, warmed jars and cover the surfaces with waxed paper discs, waxed sides down. Allow to cool before topping the jars with pieces of cellophane or airtight lids. MAKES ABOUT 1 KG/2 LB

Mincemeat

Bridget Jones

225 g/8 oz seedless raisins
225 g/8 oz sultanas
225 g/8 oz currants
225 g/8 oz shredded suet
100 g/4 oz chopped mixed peel
100 g/4 oz blanched almonds
450 g/1 lb cooking apples
1 large carrot
grated rind and juice of 1 orange
juice of 2 lemons
225 g/8 oz dark soft brown sugar
½ teaspoon freshly grated nutmeg
½ teaspoon ground cinnamon
150 ml/¼ pint brandy or rum
4 tablespoons dry sherry

Mince or finely chop the raisins, sultanas and currants and mix them with the suet and peel in a large bowl. Chop the almonds and add them to the fruit. Peel, core and grate the apples and grate the carrot, then stir both into the fruit with the orange rind and juice, the lemon juice and sugar.

Stir in the spices and pour over the brandy or rum and the sherry, mixing throughly to combine all the ingredients. Leave the mincemeat to stand for a couple of days, stirring it every day. Transfer it to pots and cover these with airtight lids. Allow to mature for at least 3 weeks before use. MAKES ABOUT 1.75 KG / 4 LB

Bramble Jelly

Bridget Jones

2.25 kg/5 lb blackberries
3 lemons
600 ml/1 pint water
sugar

Pick over and rinse the blackberries. Place them in a large saucepan. Squeeze the juice from the lemons and add it to the pan. Chop the remainder of the lemons and stir them into the blackberries.

Pour in the water and bring to the boil. Reduce the heat, cover the pan and simmer the fruit for 1 to 1½ hours, until reduced to a pulp. Allow to cool, strain through a jelly bag overnight and measure the resulting extract.

Pour the extract into a large saucepan and add 450 g/ 1 lb sugar for each 600 ml/1 pint. Heat slowly until the sugar has dissolved, stirring continuously, then bring to a rapid boil and boil hard to setting point.

Skim the surface of the jelly with a slotted spoon to remove all the scum and pour it into warmed jars. Cover the surfaces with waxed discs, waxed sides down, and allow to cool. Top the pots with lids or cellophane.

Elder and Gooseberry Jelly

—— Elizabeth Pomeroy ——

1.75 kg/4 lb green gooseberries
600 ml–1 litre/1–1¾ pints water
sugar
4–8 elder flower heads according to size

Cover the gooseberries with water – there is no need to top and tail them – then simmer the fruit, uncovered, for about 2 hours. Strain the gooseberries through a jelly bag, preferably overnight.

To each 600 ml/1 pint of juice add 450 g/1 lb warmed sugar. Heat gently, stirring, until the sugar has dissolved. Tie the elder flowers in a muslin bag and add them to the syrup. Heat to boiling point and boil briskly for 10 minutes until setting point is reached. Remove the elder flowers, pot the jelly and cover.

Honey Marmalade

—— Bridget Jones ——

4 large lemons
1.15 litres/2 pints water
675 g/1½ lb sugar
225 g/8 oz thick honey

Slice the lemons lengthways into quarters, discarding the pips, and cut the quarters widthways into fine slices. Place the fruit in a large saucepan with the water and bring the mixture to the boil. Cover the pan, reduce the heat and simmer for 1½ hours.

Add the sugar and honey and stir the mixture over a low heat until the sugar has completely dissolved. Bring it to the boil and boil rapidly until setting point is reached.

Carefully remove the scum from the surface of the marmalade with a slotted spoon, then allow it to stand for about 15 minutes. Stir the preserve thoroughly before pouring it into warmed pots. Cover the surfaces immediately with discs of waxed paper, waxed sides down, and leave to cool. Top with pieces of cellophane or airtight lids. MAKES ABOUT 1.5 KG/3 LB

Note: To make a fine marmalade, begin by paring the rind from the lemons and shredding it finely. Squeeze out the juice and place it in the pan with the rind. Chop the remainder of the fruit, tie it securely with the pips in a piece of muslin and add this to the pan. Pour in the water, bring to the boil and continue as above, but before you add the sugar, allow the marmalade to cool until the muslin can be handled. Squeeze the juices from the bag into the marmalade, pour in the sugar and proceed as in the main recipe.

Dark Orange and Lemon Marmalade

—— Bridget Jones ——

2 large oranges
4 large lemons
1.75 litres/3 pints water
1 kg/2 lb sugar
225 g/8 oz muscovado sugar

Finely chop the fruit, removing the pips, and place it in a large saucepan with the water. Bring to the boil, cover the pan and reduce the heat. Simmer for 1½ hours.

Add all the sugar to the pan and stir the mixture over a low heat until the sugar has completely dissolved. Bring to a rolling boil and continue to boil until setting point is reached.

Remove the scum from the surface of the marmalade with a slotted spoon. Allow it to stand for 15 minutes. Stir the marmalade, transfer it to heated pots and cover the surfaces with waxed paper discs, waxed sides down. When quite cool, top with pieces of cellophane and label the pots. MAKES ABOUT 1.75 KG/4 LB

Lime Marmalade

—— Bridget Jones ——

6 limes
2 lemons
1.4 litres/2½ pints water
1.5 kg/3 lb sugar

Cut the limes into quarters lengthways and then into long, very fine slices, removing all the pips. Cut up the lemons in the same way and mix both lots of fruit in a large saucepan. Pour in the water and bring to the boil. Cover the pan, reduce the heat and simmer for 1½ hours.

Add the sugar to the softened fruit and stir the mixture over a low heat until the sugar has completely dissolved. Bring the marmalade to a rolling boil and continue to boil until setting point is reached.

Remove the scum from the surface of the marmalade with a slotted spoon. Leave it to stand for 10 minutes. Stir it thoroughly before potting it in warmed jars. Top each with a disc of waxed paper, waxed side down, and leave to cool. Cover with pieces of cellophane and label the cold marmalade. MAKES 2.25 KG/5 LB

Sweet Vinegar Pickles

— Marguerite Patten —

**a selection of fresh vegetables (for example
cauliflower, pickling onions and
ridge cucumbers)
allow 1 tablespoon pickling spices to each
600 ml/1 pint white vinegar
sugar**

Choose good quality, firm vegetables which are not
discoloured. Prepare them according to their type, cut
large vegetables into small pieces and place them in a
large bowl. Sprinkle generously with salt and leave to
stand overnight. Drain, rinse and dry thoroughly.

Place the vinegar and spices in a saucepan, bring to the
boil and simmer for 15 minutes. Strain the vinegar and
sweeten it to taste with sugar. Pack the vegetables into
jars and pour in the vinegar, making sure there is enough
to cover the vegetables. Cover tightly.

Pickled Red Cabbage

— Marguerite Patten —

**1 red cabbage
salt
spiced vinegar**

Shred the cabbage, discarding any damaged outer leaves,
and layer it with salt in a large bowl. Leave to stand
overnight, drain, rinse and dry thoroughly.

Pack the cabbage loosely into jars and cover with cold
spiced vinegar. Cover tightly and use within 10 weeks as
the colour often fades.

Tomato Chutney

— Marguerite Patten —

1 teaspoon pickling spices
225 g/8 oz onions, finely chopped
300 ml/½ pint vinegar
225 g/8 oz cooking apples, peeled, cored and
chopped
1 kg/2 lb green or red tomatoes, peeled and
sliced
½ teaspoon salt
¼ teaspoon pepper
1 rounded teaspoon dry mustard
½ teaspoon ground ginger
225 g/8 oz sultanas
225 g/8 oz sugar

Put the pickling spices into a piece of muslin. Put the onions into a saucepan with 2 to 3 tablespoons of the vinegar, and simmer gently until nearly soft. Add the apples, tomatoes, spices, salt, pepper, mustard, ginger and sultanas. Simmer gently until the mixture is quite soft, stirring from time to time.

Add the remaining vinegar and the sugar. When the sugar has dissolved, boil steadily until the chutney is the consistency of jam. Remove the spices. Pour the hot chutney into warm jars and seal down at once. MAKES ABOUT 1.75 KG/4 LB

Mustard Pickles

— Marguerite Patten —

1 kg/2 lb prepared mixed vegetables (for
example, cauliflower, onions, cucumber,
small green tomatoes and green beans)
salt
600 ml/1 pint vinegar
1 tablespoon pickling spices
1 tablespoon dry mustard
2 teaspoons turmeric
50 g/2 oz sugar
1 tablespoon plain flour *or* 2 teaspoons
cornflour
2 teaspoons ground ginger

Cut or break the vegetables into small pieces (about 2.5 cm/1 in). Place in a bowl and sprinkle generously with salt, then leave to stand overnight. Wash well under cold water and drain thoroughly.

Boil the vinegar and pickling spices together steadily for 10 minutes. Mix all the dry ingredients with a very little vinegar to make a smooth paste. Pour in the strained hot vinegar, and stir well. Return to the pan, and cook until just thickened. Add the vegetables and cook for a further 5 minutes. Pour into sterilized jars and cover tightly.

Apple Chutney

— Bridget Jones —

1.5 kg/3 lb cooking apples
450 g/1 lb onions
50 g/2 oz seedless raisins
50 g/2 oz fresh root ginger
1 small green pepper
1 tablespoon dry mustard
2 teaspoons ground coriander
3 cloves garlic, crushed
275 g/10 oz demerara sugar
600 ml/1 pint vinegar

Peel, core and chop the apples, chop the onions and raisins and grate the ginger. Remove the stalk, seeds and pith from the pepper and chop the flesh. Mix all these prepared ingredients together in a large saucepan, add the mustard, coriander, garlic and sugar and pour in the vinegar.

Bring the mixture to the boil, stirring occasionally so that all the ingredients are thoroughly combined. Cover the pan, reduce the heat and simmer for 1 hour. Stir the ingredients frequently during cooking to make sure they do not stick to the pan.

Transfer the chutney to warmed pots and cover immediately with lids. Allow to mature for a few weeks if possible. MAKES ABOUT 2.25 KG/5 LB

Cucumber Relish

— Carol Bowen —

2 large cucumbers
1 head celery
1 large red pepper
1 large green pepper
450 g/1 lb onions
2 spring onions
900 ml/1½ pints white vinegar
1 teaspoon curry powder
1 teaspoon dry mustard
½ teaspoon cayenne pepper
½ teaspoon paprika
½ teaspoon ground ginger
450 g/1 lb granulated sugar

Wash the cucumbers and cut into short lengths. Scrub and trim the celery. Discard the core and seeds from the peppers and cut them into quarters. Peel and quarter the onions. Chop the spring onions, then pass all the prepared ingredients through a mincer.

Put the vinegar in a heavy-based saucepan with the spices. Bring to the boil. Add the minced ingredients and sugar and bring back to the boil. Simmer the relish for 20 to 30 minutes, until thick. Cool, pot and cover. MAKES ABOUT 2 KG / 4½ LB

Index